PHILOSOPHICAL AP

Ms. PANKAJINI BEHERA

CONTENTS

CHAPTER	TITLE	PAGE
	INTRODUCTION	1-12
1	RELIGION AND PHILOSOPHY 1.1. MEANING AND AIM 1.2. ORIGIN OF RELIGION 1.3. MAJOR RELIGIONS	13-48
2	ARGUMENTS FOR THE EXISTENCE OF GOD 2.1. COSMOLOGICAL ARGUMENT 2.2. ONTOLOGICAL ARGUMENT 2.3. TELEOLOGICAL ARGUMENT 2.4. RELIGIOUS EXPERIENCE	49-74
3	RELIGIOUS KNOWLEDGE AND LANGUAGE 3.1. RELIGIOUS LANGUAGE 3.2. RELIGIOUS SYMBOLS 3.3. RELIGIOUS HERMENEUTICS	75-99
4	DIVERSITY OF RELIGION 4.1. RELIGIOUS EXCLUSIVISM 4.2. RELIGIOUS INCLUSIVISM 4.3. RELIGIOUS PLURALISM 4.4. RELIGIOUS RELATIVISM	100-128
5	IMPLICATIONS OF RELIGION 5.1. RELIGION AND SCIENCE 5.2. RELIGION AND MORALITY	129-160
	CONCLUSION	161-172
	NOTES	173-179

CHAPTER - 1

PHILOSOPHY AND RELIGION

1.1. MEANING AND AIM

Philosophy is known as *"darśana"* in India. In the West, the Greek word "philosophy" means "love of wisdom". Philosophy all over the world (in India, China, Japan, the West, Africa, etc.) analyzes and examines three main categories: the transcendental Reality/Truth/Absolute/Brahman/God/First Cause/Causeless Cause; the conscious creatures (*jivas/cit*/soul) and the non-conscious phenomena (*jagat/acit*/matter) constituting the material world (*jagat*); for interpreting their nature, number and inter-relation through different systems of philosophy thereby formulating philosophical systems advocating – materialism, naturalism, realism, absolutism, idealism, socialism, marxism, existentialism, phenomenology, post-modernism, etc.

The word "religion" is etymologically derived from the Latin word *"religio"* meaning "obligation/bond" and *"religare"* meaning "to tie/unite/bind". Since there was no religion existing when, in ancient times, Hinduism originated as a way of life, we can use the word *"Dharma"* in the Indian context as a synonym for the religion of the Hindus. The word *"Dharma"* used to signify "religion" is a very wide term denoting duty (*e.g.* It is the *dharma* of a son to take care of his parents); ethics (*e.g.* It is the *dharma* of human beings to practice non-violence); religion (*e.g.* Nagarjuna followed Bauddha *dharma.*); mark/attribute (*e.g.* Smoke is the *dharma* of fire.); nature/essence (*e.g.* Sweetness is the *dharma* of sugar.). According to Indian philosophy, *"dharma"* is that which "binds/sustains" (*dhāranāt iti dharma*). Indian philosophy uses another word *"mata"* meaning view/opinion, commonly as a synonym for religion (*e.g.* Which *mata/religion* do you belong to?). This means that, according to Hinduism, *mata/religion*, is only a view/idea/opinion upheld by a person depending upon one's *darśana*/vision/view of Reality. Therefore, there is no one and only one right view of Reality because It/Reality/Truth/Absolute/God is infinite. This infinitude of Reality enables human beings to visualize It in a myriad ways: with form and without form, (fe)male, having name and being nameless, *etc.*; as imagined and desired by a devotee as one's chosen deity (*Iṣṭa-Devata*). Hence, the reason why the *Vedas* proclaim that Truth is one;

but, it is called by different names by the wise (*ekam sat vipraha bahuda vadanti*)! Acknowledging this aspect of Reality has enabled a catholic Hindu to worship Lord Rama in a Temple; Jesus Christ – the Saviour, in a Church; and the Almighty Allah - in a Mosque; and still continue to remain a faithful staunch Hindu, sans fanaticism!

The term "religion" has been used in two senses: (1) a narrow sense which means belief in a personal God/*Īśvara* – as the creator, controller, moral governor of the universe, who is the object of one's worship and devotion, and with whom one can communicate for attaining salvation; e.g. Judaism, Christianity, Islam, Vaiṣṇavism, Śaivism, *etc*. And, (2) a wider sense which denotes systems of thought admitting the concept of liberation/salvation. This is how the atheistic Godless schools of philosophy, *e.g.* Jainism and Buddhism, which reject the concept of God get recognized as world religions because they admit the concept of liberation – *nirvāṇa/mukti*, as the goal of human life. Thus, religion – theism (in the narrow sense) becomes a means to the attainment of religion – liberation/salvation (in the wider sense).

Philosophy and religion are grounded in human nature; the sole difference between them is that while philosophy arises from a need to comprehend, religion owes its origin to the aspiration for the Infinite. Philosophy engages one in rational or critical reflection on human goals and values, the procedures for attaining these; whereas religion springs from the compelling need to merge with the Infinite. The invocation - Oh! Lord, take me from untruth to truth (*asatomā sadgamaya*), darkness to light (*tamasomā jyotirgamaya*), mortality to immortality (*mṛtyormā amṛtamgamaya*), articulates this inherent urge which most often takes the form of religious pursuit.

Philosophy arises from one's curiosity to identify the First Cause (*tad ekam*), whereas religion originates from the practical need to attain It - the First Cause - the state of supreme fulfillment. Therefore, philosophy and religion as theory and praxis are absolutely essential for human beings. Religious pursuits assume different forms such as monotheism, polytheism, henotheism, ranging from nature worship to ideation on idols and symbols. Unconditional allegiance to authority and dogmas, and conviction in the infallibility of scriptures are the hallmarks of the religious.

Philosophizing is an endeavour, a critical task for knowing or understanding. Religion too is concerned with knowing - attaining knowledge of the Ultimate; here, 'to know' means 'to be'. But for a philosopher 'to know' means to understand. For a philosopher, reason is the guide, search-light, for understanding any phenomenon with utmost precision and clarity. Philosophic temper revolts against anything that reins human mind or stifles the free flow of reason. The goal of religious pursuit is differently conceptualized as the state of supreme good, absolute contentment and bliss, union with God; whereas the avowed objective of philosophizing is to eliminate every iota of ambiguity for achieving clarity. In philosophy, there is no room for faith or unconditional allegiance to authority. Reason takes us far and is necessary for conducting transactions in the world, but it is utterly inadequate and self-defeating when employed beyond its legitimate scope.

Revelation/scripture and authority (*āpta-vākya*) are the chief sources of religious knowledge. But, for a philosopher, knowledge is the end result of critical thinking – pure speculation (*yukti*) and reasoning (*tarka*), which the defenders of religious ontology discard due to inherent inadequacy of reason for knowing the Ultimate. For a philosopher, however, reason is the unfailing companion to know the truth, because it is assumed that reality at the core is rational and there is nothing which is beyond the scope of reason, so it is assumed, there cannot be anything which is in principle unknowable.

Thus, philosophy and religion differ from each other with regard to their objectives and methods. But there are significant ways in which religion stands in need of philosophy and philosophy can ally with religion because certain basic concepts and issues are common to both. An introspective devout follower of a religion; questions certain phenomena which appear to be anomalous and certain conceptual or theoretical issues intriguing. Here reason provides greater clarity about the goal, path, concepts and doctrines of religion. It helps one to move with greater conviction and constancy towards the cherished religious goal. All forms of rational reflection on concepts, truths and issues in religion fall within the ambit of philosophy of religion.[1]

1.2. ORIGIN OF RELIGION

The initial thought and question is what is religion all about? The answers are a belief connecting the spiritual nature of (wo)man to a supreme Being on whom one consciously depends, a Being which is self-subsistent and self-existent, it also involves practices that arise from an out of the recognition of such a relation including the personal life and experience, the principles, the rites, and the duties, associated with it. Philosophers of religion have identified different phases or mutations in the evolution of religion as follows: (1) Animism or hylozoism (2) polytheism embracing their anthropomorphism (3) Monistic religions, as Brahmanism, Confucianism, Zoroastrianism, (4) individualistic religions, as Buddhism, Mohammedanism and Christianity, etc. It would be my endeavour to show how all these various forms and the different phases of religion, originated from three sources, and also to explain the simultaneous corresponding human progress with that of one's religious ideas.

The earliest forms of religion can be found only when we study the anthropological ethnology of ancient human beings. Propitiating the elemental powers was the first origin of religion. The earliest mode of worship recognizable was of three kinds: (1) Propitiation of the superhuman powers, which was necessarily elemental, but, through anthropomorphism assumed a living form; and was the object of propitiation, invocation and solicitation, for instance, it was the propitiation of the power in the thunderstorm and not the thunderstorm per se. Primitive man due to his lack of apprehension of the various forces of nature, postulated myths, each at first was known by a sign or a symbol which later on assumed a particular deity with specific attributes.

(2) The propitiation of the spirits of the ancestors, i.e., ancestral worship, arose out of a desire for the hereafter, or an afterlife, which is based on the idea of the resurrection of the spirit. Hence, it was the propitiation of the ancestral spirit and not the body corpus of the deceased. The soul could not, and never died, but returned assuming a different name and form. And, it was due to this reason that human beings were so sure of an afterlife; and, upon this, religion was later founded.

(3) The third was the propitiation, invocation, and worship of a Great Spirit whom the primitives could not define. Thus, we find that the origin of religion is threefold. Firstly, the elemental powers were propitiated; secondly, ancestors were invoked and propitiated, and, thirdly, propitiation, invocation, and worship were made to the Great Spirit. The Gods and Goddesses of the oldest races were developed from the superhuman nature powers which originated from the earth, as the universal Great Mother. [2]

Historical Development

It is not possible to philosophize about religion unless we have sufficient knowledge of its history. We must attempt to analyze the whole religious development of humankind in all stages and phases of civilization.

Dravidian Legacy (C. 3000-2000 B.C.)

The Dravidians have made significant contribution to Indian culture and religion; and, their influence can be traced in the present Hindu religion. The discovery of Mohenjo-daro provides us with seals, figurines, stone-images, etc. which stand testimony to their religious beliefs, practices, etc. The cult of the Divine Mother and the worship of Pasupati was widely prevalent during the Indus Valley Civilization. People believed in a fertility Goddess as the source of all creation and it is reminiscent of other equivalent figures in the Mediterranean and ancient Middle Eastern religions. There are also instances of a horned God, in the posture of a yogi with two heels touching. There are also representations of nude male figurines standing upright, which is again reminiscent of later Jain statues. One need not exaggerate to say that the cult of Shiva and his consort, the practice of yoga and other kindred forms, date from this pre-historic culture.

Animism

In addition to the worship of Shiva and Shakti, both in human and symbolic forms, and the worship of demi-gods, people followed animism. Animism is a belief in highly personalized spirits inhering in natural objects, for instance, in trees, rivers, stones etc. Animal worship was part of their religious belief, and it is indicated by the representation of animals like elephant, lion, bull, buffalo in amulets and seals, or in terracotta, and stone figures.

Totemism

Totemism refers to a system in which a person or a social group is identified in a special relation with an animal or a plant or an inanimate object and the belief and customs associated with these objects. The totem is not exactly a God but a cognate being and one to be respected. The eminent sociologist, Durkheim regards it as the most simple and primitive religion. Totemism is not a universal tribal religion since there are large parts of the world where no traces of totemism have been found. Few customs, emotion and thought of tribes are involved in the totems; thus, strictly speaking, it is not a religion.

Vedic Religion (C. 2000 - 6000 B.C.)

The civilization of the Aryans, particularly their philosophical thought and religious practices during the first one thousand years is codified in the *Vedas*. The *Vedas* are the oldest Indo-European literary accomplishments; and the early Vedic religion consisted of a highly developed mythology. The word *Veda* comes from *"vid"* meaning to know; it signifies knowledge *par excellence,* and sacred wisdom. According to ancient belief, the *Vedas* are eternal, uncreated and beginningless. For *Sayana,* the *Veda* is a book describing the transcendent means for the attainment of good life and warding off evil. The *Vedas* are divided into two parts, namely: the *Jñāna-kānda*, constituted of the *Aranyakas* and the *Upaniṣads*; and the *Karma-kānda,* constituted of the *Samhitas/Mantras* and the *Brāhmaṇas.* There are four Vedas: the *Rg-Veda*, the oldest, is mainly composed of propitiatory hymns. The *Yajur Veda,* has two variants- the *Sukla-yajur-Veda* and the Kṛṣṇa-*Yajur-Veda,* consisting of sacrificial formulae. The *Sama Veda* consists of divine rhapsodies. And, the *Atharva Veda,* is comprised of magical formulae. Each Veda has four sections, namely; (i) *Samhitas* or *Mantras*- derived by *Yaska* through, thinking *manana*. This section is composed of hymns, prayers, benedictions, sacrificial formulae and litanies; (ii) *Brāhmaṇas* or prose treatises discuss the significance and meaning of sacrificial rites and ceremonies; (iii) the *Araṇyakas* deal with those who continue studying as celibates and are called *aranas* or *aranamanas*. The *Araṇas* lived in forests (*aranyas*); their speculations make up the *Araṇyakas*.

The *Upaniṣads* are works of various authors living in different ages. They are the utterances of spirituality minded people who obtained glimpses of the highest truths by earnest meditation. Their process is intensive rather than logical, and their object is to satisfy the natural yearnings of the human mind for an ultimate knowledge of the reality about God, man and the world around us. *Upaniṣads* have influenced Indian thought and philosophy considerably. All the philosophical systems and religions of India have sprung from the *Upaniṣads*. The six systems of Indian philosophy are as a whole an extension of the *Upaniṣads*. Each has its textual presentation in the highly condensed sutra pattern with a distinct commentarial collection. Vedic thinking found its maturation in the *Upaniṣads*. *Upaniṣads* are otherwise called as Vedanta as they not only constitute the concluding portions of *Vedas* (*vedas anta*) but mark the culmination of *Vedic* reflections. The *Vedas*, *Vedangas* along with dharmasastras (ordinances of Manu), the Bhagavad Gita, epics (Mahabharata and Ramayana) and eighteen *puranas* constitute *Smriti*. Vedas are claimed to be '*apuruseya*' which means 'authorless'. The truths contained in them are of the nature of revelations to the seers. Truth is eternal and impersonal. The seers were mere perceivers of truth (*rsayah mantra drastarah*). As the truths contained in them were too very profound and pithy, they were not accessible to the laity. The *Upaniṣads*, *Brahmasutra* (the compilation of the *Vedic* passages by *Vyasa*) and the Bhagavad Gita constitute three authoritative texts (*prasthana trayi*) of Hinduism.

The system of Vedanta, however, constitutes a special and self-complete exposition of the message of the *Upaniṣads*. Of the other systems, the *Purva Mimamsa* is closest to Vedanta with a claim for chronological priority. Dealing directly with the *Karma-Kanda* of the Vedas and containing an exposition of the *Jamini*-sutras, even as the system of Vedanta contains an exposition of the Vyasa-sutra, the *Purva-Mimansa* and *Uttara-Mimansa* would together exhaust the practical and the intensive speculative aspects of the *Veda-Vedanta* heritage. The other four systems are not directly concerned with a comprehensive exposition of the substance of the *Upaniṣads*.

The major *Upaniṣads* must have pre-existed the rise of the six systems of Indian philosophy. The main theme of the *Upaniṣads* is the spiritual unity of all existence. This is clearly reflected in the opening verse of the *Ishavasya- Upaniṣads,* which is generally recognized as the oldest. "*Isha-Vasyam idam sarvam*" conveys the idea that one supreme, omnipresent reality of the entire cosmic scheme is hailed as *Isha* or the supreme ruler. The *Kena- Upaniṣads* illumines the nature of knowledge by contrasting sense-knowledge and knowledge of ultimate reality, which transcends sense-knowledge. The *Katha- Upaniṣads* reflects a happy blends of mysticism and philosophy, and breathes the pure fragrance of sublime poetry. The Katha contains what has been described by Sri Aurobindo as a unified exposition of Vedanta. *Mundaka Upaniṣads* draws an initial distinction between '*paravidya*' (higher knowledge) and '*apara vidya*' (lower knowledge). The *Mandukya Upaniṣads* analyses the *pranava mantra,* AUM. One of the "*Mahavakyas*" or lofty and sublime utterances "*Ayem Atma Brahma*", "this Atma (the self of man) is Brahman" occurs in the Mandukya. While the *Taittiriya* contains some of the most significant utterances, like "*Brahma-Vidaproti Param*" "*Satyam jnanam Anantam Brahma*", the *Aitareya* has the second vakya to its credit, "*Prajnanam Brahma*" meaning "Brahma is pure consciousness".

The *Chandogya* and the *Brihadaranyaka* Upanisads provide ample scope for spiritual perfection with its Vedic symbolism and Vedantic intention. To the Chandogya belongs that classic declaration of superlative significance, "Tattvamsi" (that thou art), and to the *Brihadaranyaka* the other philosophical utterance "*Aham Brahmasmi*" (I am Brahman).[3]

1.3. MAJOR WORLD RELIGIONS

1.3.1. HINDUISM

Hinduism is the most ancient religion of the world. It is a complex labyrinth of beliefs, myths, rituals, prescriptions and prohibitions. Hinduism refers to the religion of the Āryāns who in the beginning were polytheists; but, in due course of time, posited one transcendental God (*Prajāpati* or *Viśvakarma* or *Hiraṇyagarbha*) at the centre-stage, with other Gods and Deities, subordinate to Him.

Hinduism is also known as *Sanātan Dharma*. 'Sanātana', literally means that which is beginningless. The *Vedas* are the foundational scriptures of the Hindus. The four *Vedas*; *Ṛg.*,*Yajur, Sāma*, and *Atharva*, constitute the basis for the six *Vedāṅgas*, which literally means 'limbs of the *Vedas*'. These were the six auxiliary disciplines connected with the *Vedas* that developed in ancient Vedic culture. They are, (i) S*ikṣā* (science of pronunciation, phonetics, phonology), (ii) *Chhandas* (prosody;metre), (iii) *Vyākaraṇa* (grammar and linguistic analysis), (iv) *Jyotiṣa* (astronomy),(v) *Kalpa* (sacred ordinance about the use of *mantra*), and (vi) *Nirukta* (etymology). Sāṅkhya, Yoga, Nyāya, Vaiśesika, Mīmāṁsā and Vedānta constitute the six philosophies orthodox (*darśanas*) pledging their allegiance to the *Vedas*. The *Vedas* are also called *sṛuti*, because they are sacred knowledge or divine revelation passed down, from generation to another through oral transmission. The word '*Upaniṣad*' is derived from *upa*(near), *ni* down and *sad* to sit). The *Upaniṣads* explain the mystic significance of the syllable *Aum*, and mystical words such as *Tajjalān*, which are accessible only to the initiated. *Saṅkara* derived the word "*Upaniṣad*" as a substantive from the root '*sad*,' to loosen' 'to reach' 'to destroy', with *upa* and *ni* as prefixes and *kvip* as termination. (In his commentary on the *Taittiriya Upaniṣad*, he says, *upanisannam va asyam param śreya iti*). If one accepts this definition, *Upaniṣad* signifies *Para-Vidya*, which destroys ignorance. *Upaniṣads* are also called Vedānta because they not only constitute the concluding portion of *Vedas* (*vedasya anta*) but mark the culmination of Vedic metaphysics. The Vedas, Vedāṅgas along with *Dharmasātras* (Ordinances of Manu), the *Bhagavad Gitā*, Epics(*Mahābhārata* and *Rāmāyaṇa*) and theeighteen Purāṇas constitute *Smṛti*. The *Vedas* are claimed to be '*apuruṣeya*' which literally means "authorless", and the Vedic truths are revelations of the seers, who perceived the eternal and impersonal truths (*ṛsayah mantra drastārah*). Hence, there was the need for *Kāvyas* (epics) and *Purāṇas* to present these abstract truths in a manner intelligible to the commoners. The *Upaniṣads*, The *Brahma-sūtra* (the compilation of the Vedic passages by Vyāsa) and the *Bhagavad-Gitā* constitute the three authoritative texts (*prasthāna-Traya*) of Hinduism.

The Vedic pantheon is over populated by Gods and deities, so diverse and complex in their power and scope that it becomes almost impossible to arrive at a definitive notion of God. The monotheistic creeds and practices revolving around Lord Siva (Saivism), Lord Kṛṣṇa (Vaiṣṇavism) and cosmic energy (Sakti cult) demand their followers to remain non-compromisingly loyal to their God.

Hindus by and large, are polytheistic in their belief; but, monotheistic in practice. One discerns the persistent tendency in Vedic thinking towards monotheism as there are musings, taking Prajāpati, Viśvakarma and Hiranyagarbha as cosmic deities. Polytheism and monotheism of different forms are accommodated within Hinduism. Belief in one Reality (monism) known by different names (*ekam sat viprah bahuda vadanti*) is the soul and substance of Hinduism. The ultimate reality is Brahman which is one without a second (*ekam eva advitīyam*).

Brahman is of the nature of existence – knowledge bliss (*sat-cit-ānanda*) : Brahman is Sat because it is non- sublatable in principle; *Cit* in the sense that it is of the nature of pure consciousness, and *Ānanda* refers to the state of infinite bliss. Brahman, in its unmanifested (*avyakta*) state, is attributeless (*nirguṇa*); and, in its manifested form has attributes (*saguṇa*). Brahman and Īśvara (God) are implicit and explicit states of the same Being. Brahman, by its creative potency, plays the role of God (*Īśvara*), who is the creator, preserver, and destroyer in relation to the universe. He is beyond time, space and causality. God is the both the efficient and the material cause (*nimitta-upādāna-kāraṇa)* of the universe. Hence, it is rightly said,

He is the maker of all, the knower of all, the self-caused, the knower, the author of time. He is to be seen as beyond the three kinds of time (past, present and future). This indemonstrable and constant being can be realised as one only. The self is taintless, beyond space, unborn, great and constant. He is the beginning, the source of the causes which unite the soul with the body.

Brahman is both transcendent and immanent; as the transcendent entity, it is beyond space, time causality, beyond thought and language. It is neither fine nor gross, neither long nor short …unattached, without eyes, without smell, without voice, without ears, without mind, without measure, breath or mouth. It eats nothing and no one eats it. Brahman is infinite; it is infinitely, bigger than the biggest, and smaller than the smallest.

"It is the essence of every creature. Through tranquillity of the mind and the senses, a person can realize the greatness of the self".

As pure consciousness, Brahman is the precondition of all knowledge. Hence, Brahman cannot be known. "Knowledge" presupposes the distinction between knower and the known, subject and the object. Brahman is Infinite, so, how can the "infinite" be object of knowledge when the knower is 'finite'? It does not amount to agnosticism for it simply means that Brahman cannot be known in the way other particulars and objects are known. Hence, the *Upaniṣads* advocate knowing by becoming. When the knower knows the object by becoming it, the knower of Brahman becomes Brahman. As the immanent principle, it is the essence of every particular. Therefore, it resists any attempt at describing it through finite predicates.

There are scholars who emphasize the attributed or personal (*saguna*) aspect of Brahman i.e. *Īśvara*. The ultimate Reality can be ideated upon, prayed, loved only in its personal aspect. Thus, the theistic systems evolved, keeping God (*Īśvara / Bhagavān*) as the focal point of their ethico-spiritual endeavour. Ramanuja takes *Īśvara* (God) as the soul of the conscious (*cit*) and the non-conscious(*acit*) phenomena which constitute the world. And, the *Īśvara*-soul/world relation is called *śarīra-śarīri-bhāva*. God-realization is possible only through devotion (*bhakti*) which consists in constant remembrance of God. *Īśvara* manifests Himself through creation, preservation and destruction. As creator He is Brahma, as preserver Viṣnu and as destroyer Siva. They are not three independent entities but One God in three different roles discharging different functions.

The creation of the world is traced to the desire of the One (Brahman) to become many, God does not create the world as an external agent; rather He creates the many by becoming the many. Brahman, the macro-cosmic consciousness, having created the world, resides as the very essence of every particular and conceals Himself within, as the inner Self. Every created object is potentially conscious and partakes of the nature of the ultimate Reality. The primeval universe is characterized as both non-existent (*asat*) in the sense that there was no existence of any particular whatsoever; and as existent (*sat*) in the sense that all the possibilities resided in the state of substantive consciousness (Brahman).

Hindu cosmogony, by and large, rests on the fundamental view that the One evolves into the many; and the many relapse into the One. The beginning and the end of evolution is one and the same. At the core, there is the One self-same consciousness, appearing as the many, just as air which is formless assumes different forms, depending on the nature of the bubble in which it resides.[4] Accordig to Advaita the world is considered as neither real nor non-real (*anīrvacanīya*) *sadāsad vilakṣaṇa*; and any logical understanding of it, is bound to be disappointing. It is illusory (*mithyā*) because it is relative, contingent, impermanent and subject to sublation (*bādha*). But our experience of the world, characterized by awareness of its diversities, disappears when one realises the ultimate Truth (*Pāramārthika Sat*), whereby one sees only the One - Brahman, as the singular continuum in and through all varied phenomena.

Like any other existent or being, (wo) man partakes of the nature of the Divine. But, unlike other phenomena, consciousness (the immanent principle in every-existent) is most explicitly manifest in human beings. (Wo) man can not only reflect on the whys and how's of creation, but also make conscious and concerted effort to attain the goal, variously termed as *mokṣa*/*mukti*/*apoha*/*paramārtha,* etc. (Wo)man is caught between two opposing forces: one that creates irresistible urge to attain the state of bliss; and, the other which makes one move away from the destined goal, termed as *vidyā*, and *avidyā* respectively. Where *vidyā* is liberative (*sāvidyā yā vimuktaye*), *avidyā* leads one to the world of darkness and transmigration.

(Wo)man is a body-mind-self complex constituted the five gross elements- earth (*kṣiti*), water (*ap*), fire (*tajas*), air (*vāyu*) and ether (*ākāśa*). The body and mind are constituted of *sattva, rajas* and *tamas* - the elements of *prakṛti*. The body senses & mind are subject to birth, growth, maturation, decay and extinction. But, the self is immortal and ever pure. As one discards clothes, which are worn out, the soul too abandons the body and moves across different births when the body is worn out. Bondage of the individual is explained by the twin concepts of *maya* and *avidyā*. *Māyā* is the creative power of Brahman by which it takes on different forms and keeps itself veiled from outer view, whereas *avidyā* (nescience/ignorance) refers to the limitation of the individual because of which one fails to discover the Eternal behind the ephemeral, The absolute behind the contingent, and the spiritual behind the terrestrial. Because of *avidyā*, the individual is led to superimpose the illusory on the real. This is elucidated by the rope-snake illusion: A rope is misperceived as a snake because of similarity. The rope remains a rope all through, irrespective of one's ignorance or knowledge about it. But *māyā*, with its two powers, (*āvaraṇa śakti/supressio very*) and (*vikṣepa sakti/suggest falsi*); conceals the real (rope- Brahman) and projects the illusory (snake- *jivas* and *jagat*) as real world of names and forms (*nāma-rūpa*). The individual due to ignorance (*avidyāi*), mistakes the names and forms to be real. Thereby, the nature of Reality is not only concealed/non-apprehended but also distorted/mis-apprehended. The 'real' appears as something other than itself (*atasmintadbuddhih*). Sāṅkhya identifies three kinds of suffering; the physical and mental suffering brought about by oneself and intra-organic causes (*ādhyātmika*), others interpersonal and natural causes (*ādibhautika*) and by super natural forces such as, earthquakes, floods, tsunamis, etc. (*ādhidaivika*).

The *Law of karma* is a central tenet of Hinduism. According to it, the doer of an action is bound to reap the consequences of one's actions, not only in this life but in endless cycles of births, with accompanying pleasure and pain. There is an inter-relation between action (*karma*) and liberation (*mukti*). The doctrine of desireless/selfless action (*niskama karma*) is expounded to solve this connection. One who performs *niṣkamakarma* escapes karmic bondage. Karma binds an individual as long as one has the sense of doer-ship for achieving a personal end(*iṣta*). A *niṣkamakarmi* acts considering oneself as a mere instrument (*nimitta*). This brings about an end of the sense of a doer/agent and confers detachment for the fruit of the action. In the case of a devotee (*bhakta*) the doer is He God (Brahman/*Īśvara*, the transcendental agent), the consequences good or bad, are offered unto Him. The *Law of Karma* shows how the past, present and future are inter-connected through the karmic nexus. Each individual carries the load of one's *prārabdha* (reactions of past actions in their potential present form) which tend to fructify when congenial conditions are available. There is no room for fatalism in the law of *karma* as it states that every action is prospectively significant.

Determinism of the past holds out the hope that by choosing to act in a particular way in the present, one becomes the architect of one's own destiny.

Varṇa-dharma classifies human beings into four fundamental classes namely, *Brāhmana, Kṣatriya, Vaiśya,* and *Sūdra*. Originally, such classification was made on the basis of the predominant psychic trait of an individuals. The *Vipras/Brahmins* are predisposed to tread the path of virtues and attain enlightenment. They are a class of morally and spiritually awakened people. The *Kṣatriya* is one who is more prone to use one's physical strength. They are the warriors who can best serve the society by defending it against the onslaught of evil forces. A successful social life also needs people who have a knack and expertise in running the affairs of the world; they are the *Vaiśyas* who are inclined to pursue trade and commerce. The *Sūdras* are those who serve the other three classes and contribute their mite to the society by rendering physical service. A healthy society needs these four classes (*varṇas*) of people for its existence functioning and progress. The varṇa or class system degenerated into caste system based on inheritance and heredity resulting in social discrimination and Brāhmanical exploitation of the others.

Āśrama-dharma refers to four different stages of life such as; *Brahmacarya, Gṛhastha, Vānaprastha* and *Sanyāsa*. The period of *Brahmacarya* is the time for practising the qualities of the head and the heart and self-restraint to ensure a smooth transition to the state of a householder (*Gṛhastha*) whereof one is expected to lead a successful life as a house holder. Having discharged one's worldly obligations for one's family and society, one is supposed to lead a retired life of relative detachment and contemplation in the stage of Vānaprastha which eventually prepares one for a life of renunciation (*sannyāsa*). Hinduism does not advocate renunciation of action but renunciation in action. Life of action is not decried as a hindrance on the path to liberation. Rather, it is extolled as a rare opportunity to live a life of rectitude for attaining the state of liberation (*mukti*).

The ethics of the Hindus is based on their world-view. The world is pervaded by Brahman. Every particle of the universe is potentially infinite and is subject to the process of evolution which is of the nature of Self-discovery and unconcealment. Evolution is teleological because all beings, animate and inanimate, converge to one end which is also the source of their emergence. Since Brahman is all pervasive, ubiquitous, everyone is bound by every other by the bond of cosmic kinship. Everything is divine and everyone is a kindred. The concept of cosmic fraternity (*vasudaiva kutumbakam*) is the ethical paradigm, implied by Hindu cosmo-centric ontology. Since all the animate and the inanimate phenomena are pervaded by Brahman, the real happiness of an individual involves living for the other.

Hinduism emphasizes the importance of self-effort and the grace of God. One has to make sustained effort to progress on the path of righteousness. In personal life, Advaita exhorts one to cultivate the fourfold prerequisites (*sādhanā chatustaya*) for attaining enlightenment. They are discrimination (*viveka*) for distinguishing the eternal from the non-eternal (*nityānitya vastuviveka*). This bestows detachment (*vairāgya*) for all the world phenomena (*Iha mutrārtha bhogavirāga*). Thirdly, one has to acquire the six virtues (*ṣad sampati*) involving mind-control (*śama*), sense-control (*dama*), forbearance (*titikṣa*), withdrawal (*uparati*), faith in guru and scripture (*sraddhā*), and one pointed concentration (*samādhi*). Above all, there has to be an earnest longing for liberation (*mumukṣutva*) which involves guided study of scriptures (*śravaṇa*) rational reflection (*manana*) and contemplation (*nididhyāsana*) on the Absolute for actualizing a smooth transition from knowing to Being, bondage to liberation (*mokṣa*).

Dharma, Artha, Kama, and *Mokṣa* constitute the four values of human life (*puruṣarthas*). They spell out a modus operandi by which life in the world can be lived, desires and actions can be regulated, so that every occasion in life facilitates one's journey towards the cherished goal. *Artha* includes the material wealth. Kama denotes desire for sense-pleasures, physical and psychic wants are satiated. *Kama* and *artha* have to be regulated by *dharma* (righteousness), so that one attains *mokṣa*, the highest purusartha. *Dharma* denoting virtuous conduct derives its significance from the concept of *Ṛta*, the immanent causal uniformity (found in the state of nature) and the moral order (found in the karmic domain). When one acts in accordance with the cosmic order it is termed as righteousness (dharma). When one thinks and speaks in conformity with the cosmic order, it is called *satya*. Hence, the injunction, speak the truth (*satyam vada*), tread the path of righteousness (*dharmamchara*). Theistic religions prescribe worship and devotion. Idolatry has the tendency to degenerate into formalism and ritualism. So the individual is asked to view the idol as a representative of the ideal.

Activism (*pravṛttti*) and asceticism (*nivṛitti*) are recommended as two different paths leading to liberation. Those who are enlightened can attain Brahmanhood by practising restrain of renunciation and inward contemplation. On the other hand, those who are subject to the compulsions of life have to follow the way of activism (*pravṛtti-marga*) through karma-yoga, so that every moment that is lived becomes a preparation and a step forward the attainment of Brahman. Though, knowledge (*jnana*), action (*karma*), and devotion (*bhakti*) are declared as independent paths to the highest Reality by different schools of philosophy, the three are construed as complementary. That is why the synthesis of knowledge, action and devotion (*jñāna-karma-bhakti samuccaya*) is mooted as the most potent way to liberation.[5]

1.3.2. CHRISTIANITY

Christianity is the largest religion of the world in terms of its influence and followers. It is rooted in the basic tenets of Judaism, and largely based on the life and teachings of Jesus, supplemented by the Apostles. The Bible is the holy book of the Christians which contains the concepts of 'Virgin Birth', 'Trinity', 'Resurrection', F*elix Culpa* and the "Day of Judgment". Jesus was born in Bethlehem to virgin mother Mary and foster father Joseph. Though a Jew by birth, his mission was to liberate his fellowmen from the narrow confines of beliefs, practices and the rigid orthodoxy which had penetrated Judaism at his time. He did not, explicitly, seek to propagate a religion of his own but only wanted to purge the non-religious accretions in the religious faith of the Jews. His interpretation of the fundamental tenets were very distinctively conspicuous that it gave birth to a new religion called 'Christianity'. His was the creed of love, compassion, forgiveness and service. The life, teachings and crucifixion of Jesus are the living testimony of the values he practiced and the religion he propagated. His radical interpretations made him appear as a non-conformist, a heretic, a renegade against the religious beliefs and practices of the day which drew the displeasure of the King, eventually leading to his crucifixion. The inklings of divinity in Jesus is revealed through his miracles like when he restored vision to the blind, cured lepers by mere touch, forgave the woman who was about to be stoned to death for committing adultery. He was accessible and endeared himself to the rich and the poor, the noble and the ignoble, believers and non-believers alike. He embraced all and detested none, irrespective of their status and doings. Above all, his prayer on the cross for those who crucified him: *"Forgive them Father,* *they do not know what they are doing*!" constitutes the bedrock of the mission, called Christianity. God incarnated himself, in flesh and blood in the person of Jesus, enable the lesser mortals experience the glory of God.

The Bible constituted of the Old Testament and the New Testament. The contents of the Old Testament are incorporations of the Hebrew texts. The New Testament consists of four Gospels which record the life and teachings of Jesus, the history from resurrection to the days of St. Paul, the sayings of the saints of Christendom and revelations to St. John.

God is one. He is omnipotent and omniscient, His creation is *ex nihilo*. He sustain and destroy it by the same. Being infinite and transcendent, he remains beyond the reach of the intellect and sensory experience. God is the creator of all that exists. He is the unconditioned world ground and everything, tiny or big, non-living or living is dependent on Him. God, the supreme Father, on account of His infinite love for His creation, especially (wo)man whom He created in the likeness of Him, sent Jesus (Son of God), to redeem humanity from sins. God had to incarnate Himself in the person of Jesus, in order to atone for the sins of humankind and redeem them from their sinful predicament. The advent of Jesus opened the gates for salvation after the first act of disobedience.

God, Jesus (Son of God) and the Holy Ghost (Holy Spirit) constitute the 'Trinity' of Christianity. The notion of 'Trinity' does not dilute monotheistic convictions of the Christians. God, the Son of God, the Holy Spirit, is not three distinct entities but threefold expressions of the same entity.

Human beings are prone to sin. God waits in the wings to forgive all sins and embrace back the repenting souls who seek forgiveness. Since God is infinite love, no sin can be too great to be not forgiven. God redeems one who grows penitent for one's sins and turns to Him for refuge. Though God, in the person of Jesus, had a personality, He was immune to the limitations of a human person. God became embodied to live the life of Divinity and eventually courted crucifixion and resurrection on the third day of His demise are all evidence of God's love for His creation.

The world was created *ex nihilo*, owes it existence to divine will, and depends on God for its continuance. God is beyond time and space because time & space become meaningful only after creation of the world and all its phenomena. God alone existed when there was nothing else. Hence, Creator remains immune to the contingency of time, space and causality, which the created world of particulars is subject to. The world was created in six days. By the first three days of the creation, there was neither the sun nor the moon. Having created light, air, water, vegetation, animals and birds, God desired to create human-beings in the likeness of Him.

The world, a handiwork of God, reflects his glory. Constancy in the functioning of nature, hierarchy in creation, laws that regulate events nature and those that determine the birth, growth decay and death of the animate are evidence for the existence of God. The world affords an opportunity to understand the will of God and live righteously by participating in His mission and fulfilling His will. Calamities like flood, famine, earthquakes, cyclones are not aberrations; they are willfully summoned by God to punish human beings for their disobedience of His commandments, and remind the mortals about the ways of God.

God created man in his own image on the final day of creation, and granted him dominion over all other phenomena and nature. Unlike other creatures, (wo)man is endowed with soul which constitutes one's spiritual nature. God wanted man to be a fellow partner in translating His will on earth, i.e., the establishment of the kingdom of God on earth. And for its accomplishment God gifted (wo)man with a knowledge of good and bad and, freewill to choose between them.

'Freewill', the most precious gift, accords the characteristics dignity to man, which enables man to choose between 'good' and 'bad'. To choose 'evil' amounts to disobedience to the will of God, and the biblical accounts relate how Adam, the first man, committed the original sin by disobeying the will of God, whereby he fell from His grace. On account of this, it is not only that he (Adam) deprived himself from the saving grace of the Father but that His descendent came to possess the sinful nature. It doesn't mean that man is eternally condemned to remain sinful and suffer eternal damnation. As by misuse of freewill he becomes fallen, by righteous use of will, he can regain his spiritual nature and get back to the abode of God which is his original home. The soul does become impure on account of sinful actions; hence, it is needful to purge it by cultivating faith in God with all one's heart, mind and soul. The highest perfection cannot be attained by self-effort, by mere exercise of creaturely freedom, but it needs the loving grace of the Father too, so that he can grow into the likeness of God. Freewill leaves open the alternatives of living the life of damnation by disobeying His will or grow into the likeness of God by living a life, according to His biddings. Unbounded faith in God, redemptive death of Jesus, intangible help of the Holy Ghost, repentance for one's sins and sincere prayer to God (seeking His forgiveness), make one worthy of God's forgiveness. Conversion does not consist merely in the formal act of being baptized but effecting transformation within, for living a life of love, service and sacrifice. Life begins with physical birth and ends with disintegration of the body. Though the body (made up matter) disintegrates, the soul survives the physical death of the person and awaits the judgement of God until the day of Resurrection. The soul is created by God, at the time of conception. It is worth noting that Christianity doesn't accept the prenatal existence of soul. The soul begins to inhabit the body at the time of conception but does not die with physical death. The righteous make proper use of life for redemption, and for partaking the glory of Heaven, whereas the wicked misuse it and are subject to eternal damnation.

Christianity is essentially a religion of love and service. Whereas God's love is infinite, human love is finite, and tainted by conditionality. Unlike human love (*Peros*), God's love (*Agape*) is unconditional. Hence, God loves all, be they sinful or virtuous. He loves us not because of what we are but irrespective of what we are. True love entails forgiveness. This is exemplified in the act of supreme sacrifice by none other than Jesus and His pronouncement.

"Love your enemies and pray for those who persecute you."

Hatred is inadmissible in Christianity, and it is to be returned with love and vengeance, with forgiveness. Every mortal ought to imbibe such love and grow into the likeness of the Father. Love generates the urge to serve with humility and stoic fortitude and service to humanity is to service to God. The best way to please the Father is to love and serve one's fellowmen because all are the offspring's of one supreme Father. God knows all that we think and do. On the Day of Judgment, Lord shall provide an account of the Samaritan acts of the persons who are redeemed.

Man is prone to err and tread the path, forbidden by God. Given the limitation of man, even 'faith' cannot be cultivated, out and out, by self-effort. In other words, "to have faith in God" is not a human feat; it is the free gift of God which accrues to the individual as loving dispensation of His grace.

Christian ethics discourages mindless pursuit of wealth. One should possess only that much which is needed for living a life of righteousness and work for the Father's mission of the Father. Earthly riches are ephemeral; one should rather accumulate the riches enabling one paradise. Accumulation beyond necessity makes one prone to pursue a path, unbecoming of man and contrary to the will of God, hence, the necessity of restraint on the acquisitive instinct which facilitates one to live the life of contemplation, love and service.[6]

1.3.3. ISLAM

Islam is a prophetic religion and shares common Semitic origin with Judaism and Christianity. "Islam" literally means submission to the will and ways of God. It acknowledges a long lineage of Prophets like Abraham, Moses, Jesus, and Muhammad-the last Prophet. *Quran* generally relates the preaching of 124,000 Prophets, and specifically about 25 Prophets. Not every prophet is a messenger God endeavored to awaken the slumbering humanity to convey the tidings of God, to enkindle hope in lesser mortals, promising Heavenly abode for those who are willing to tread the path of God, while reminding people of the dismal consequences of disobedience of His will.

Muhammad was born in Arabia in 570 A.D. and continued the message of Islam which is out and out monotheistic; it was a departure from the received beliefs and practices of the time. Islam was essentially a non-compromising crusade against prevailing contemporary polytheism, idolatry, ritualism and superstitions. Therefore, Muhammad had to face vehement opposition from the then ruling regime. At the age of forty, God revealed Himself to Muhammad through the angel Gabriel on the Mount Hīra. In the beginning, there were very few takers of his views. His wife Khadija was the first to be won over to the path which gained ground through the first Caliph Abu Bakr. Subsequently, Islam went beyond the frontiers of Arabia through royal patronage, expeditions and conquests.

Al- Quran is the sacred book of the Muslims containing the words of God (Āllah) in its pure and pristine form as revealed to Muhammad, the Messenger (*Rasul*). "*Quran*" means to recite. The revelations of God were recited by Muhammad to his followers who codified them faithfully in form of a book, the *Quran*. It consists of 114 Chapters (*Suras*) written in Arabic. It stands supported by the sayings (*Ahadis*), practices (*Hadith*) and the ethical injunctions (*Sharia*) in the form of do's and don'ts.

Islam proclaims the oneness of God in unequivocal terms: God is one and Muhammad is the Prophet, who brought home the message of God to people so that they can lead righteous life during their worldly sojourn and thereafter find a worthy place in Heaven, enjoying eternal fellowship with God. "Allah" means the "powerful mighty" and He is the creator, preserver and destroyer of the world. The world is dependent on Him and nothing takes place without His knowledge and will as He is the supreme arbiter of all that happens small or big. He is the moral governor of the cosmos and all existence is an expression of His power and glory. On the Day of Judgment, He dispenses reward and punishment to everyone according to one's deeds, during their terrestrial sojourn. Though one finds a place in Heaven or Hell due to their deeds, the choice to forgive or punish, rests eventually on Him. His ways are inscrutable, if He so wills He can reverse His own decree.

The notion of 'freewill' makes sense only in the domain of human intentions, will and actions. But the world (creation) eventually conforms to the will and ways of God. God is transcendent since He is too high and too great for man to have direct access to Him. There is an unbridgeable chasm between the creator and His creation, God and (wo)man. He is known only when He desires to reveal Himself through the mediation of Angels or directly to the Prophets in sleep or waking. God is known only when one is graced by Him. Islam is non-compromisingly opposed to idol worship and the belief in the incarnation of God in human form. That is why it is critical of the Christian view that Jesus is the son of God and their faith in the Trinity i.e. God, Son of God (Jesus) and the Holy Ghost. While claiming that God is non-physical and transcendent, it denies the immanence of God and the essential identity between (wo)man and God.

Islam admits the reality of Angels who are created from light. Unlike humans, they are non-corporeal, and do not need sustenance trough food. Again unlike human beings, they have no "freedom of will", the choicest gift of God for man. There are Angels who praise God and carry out His commands. There is also another creation called "*Jinns*" who are created out of fire. One among them is "*Iblis*" who disobeyed the God's command and tempts the mortals to tread the path of evil.

Though Islam accepts the Judaic and Christian concept of creation, in spirit, it does not admit the theory of creation *ex nihilo*. The world is created in time and comes to an end on the Day of Judgment. Creation, with its grandiose design and splendor, speaks eloquently of the creator and evokes a sense of awe and faith. It also is purportedly not an act of play but has a telos. Space and time along with creation itself is finite and contingent as they are subject to multiplicities. Since everything, tiny or big, is the handiwork of God, creation bears the unmistakable stamp of His greatness and glory. One feels His benign presence in everything that exists and happens. Nature too, follows a predetermined course at the behest of God.

(Wo)man is one of the best creations of God and occupies the highest place in the hierarchy of created phenomena. Man stands distinct to other many creations. Since human beings are endowed with freewill and the capacity to think, they have the freedom to obey the commandments of God; thereby, a person earn the Paradise for oneself or act contrarily and get condemned to Hell. As God reposes trust in (wo)man, the highest good of an individual involves living as a devout servant of God. A person has no rights but only duties and life becomes worthwhile, only when it is spent in prayer and service. In prayer, one should not to seek anything except the benign grace of God. Although human beings have an inherent capacity to rise to nobleness and glory. One can, at the most grow into the likeness of God, and live close to Him, but howsoever sincere, may be the effort and fervent, the longing, one can never become God. Islamic cosmogony envisions limited freedom for (wo)man against the backdrop of absolute divine determinism. The worst thing that can happen to a person is that, by misuse of 'freewill' one court one's own ruin because, one has hardly the ability to upset the design of God which eventually prevails.

Human personality involves a body and the indwelling soul. Life begins with physical birth but does not terminate in physical death, because the soul remains afresh till the last day when the world comes to an end and all the dead rise up, to the blowing of the trumpet and the souls reunite with the bodies. They are summoned before God by the Angels and await His final decree. One is accorded a rightful place, either in Heaven or in Hell, depending on one's deeds. There is graphic description of heaven and hell in *Quran*, it delineates seven layers of Heavenly bliss, as well as the seven stages of Hellish agony. Since human beings are free, one is at liberty either to believe or not believe, and to tread the right path or the wrong path. But as is the action, so is the reward or punishment, dispensed by Allah.

'*Pul-e-siraat*' is the bridge a soul has to cross after the pronouncement of the final judgment; it is smooth and wide for the virtuous but narrows like the edges of a sword for the wicked. The highest good of man, therefore, consists in finding a place in heaven so that one lives in perpetual fellowship with God and angels. But in that state, (wo)man continues to be finite, even though a person lives as pure spirit without the limitation of body and mind.

Since everything happens according to His design and decree, suffering has a necessary place in His scheme. Suffering could be the result of punishment for one's wrong doing or purposely sent by God to test the degree of faith and one's loyalty to God. Iblis, the devil, holds out temptations and prompts a person to commit evil. But the supreme good of an individual consists in overcoming them by making righteous use of will. Besides, evil is summoned by God so that a person can turn to God for redressal of one's suffering.[7]

A devout Muslim has five fundamental duties: (1) Faith in the ultimate truth (*Kālima*) (2) Prayer (*Namāz*) (3) Observance of fast (*Ramadan*) (4) Pilgrimage to Mecca (*Haj*) and (5) Charity (*Zakat*). Islam lays stress on living a life of faith, surrender, discipline and brotherhood. Faith is expressed in action in form of discipline and unconditional submission to God, which eventually secures one the highest good i.e. a place in Heaven. A faithful is one who not only believes but lives a life accordingly, because there should be no hiatus between one's thinking and the way one speaks and acts. Faith involves total participation of one's being and strong conviction about the truth contained in the sacred expression: *God is most high. There is no god but God (Allah) and Muhammad is His Prophet.*

Namaz: Repetition of this means repeated affirmation of faith in oneness of Allah and Muhammad as His Prophet. Constant remembrance of this truth has its necessary expression in the life of an individual and the community, at large. This forms a necessary part of the daily prayer (*Namāz*). Every Muslim has to offer prayers *Namāz* five times every day strictly, at the appointed time i.e. before sunrise, in the afternoon, before sunset, in the evening and before going to sleep, to reinforce one's faith, fortify one's conviction and serve as positive deterrent in keeping the mind away from devilish wanderings and preoccupations. While praying, one has to face towards Mecca. Mosque is a place of worship for the Muslims and these are so structured that while offering *Namāz*, the devotees face towards Mecca. Offering *Namāz,* involves in taking different postures (*raka*). Each posture represents a state of surrender to Allah. The first prayer consists of two *rakas*; the second and third consists of four *rakas*, the evening prayer, includes three and the fifth prayer consists four rakas begins with the utterance, God is the great (*Allah hu Akbar*) followed by the maiden verse (*Sura*) of Quran. Bismillah (God, the creator of Heaven and earth the most benevolent and compassionate).

The prayer ends with the utterance of the *Kalima*, "There is no God but Allah and Muhammad is His Prophet". Besides offering *Namāz* individually, participation in congregational prayer in the mosque is also regarded as a sacred duty. Mass prayers are also held on the days of "*Eid-ul-Fitr*" and "*Eid-ul-Adha*". The leader of the group called *Imam* is entrusted with the task of leading the prayer, while doing it himself before others.

Ramadan: The ninth month of the Muslim calendar is observed as *Ramadan*, the month of fasting. A Muslim has to fast for the whole month with the exception of the pregnant women, sick, old and travelers. One has to fast without food, and water between dawn and sunset. Fasting has a vital role in facilitating spiritual progress. It too has salutary effect both on the body and the mind. It does not merely involve denying oneself food and water but affords an opportunity for self-control and positive ideation on God, confess poise for contemplation, and moral rectitude.

Zakat: Besides pursuit of religious discipline in personal life, follower of Islam has to cultivate the virtue of charity (*Zakat*), by sharing one's fortunes with the less privileged ones. One has to part with five percent or ten percent on one's income by way of attending to the needy and poor, depending on one's capacity and circumstances. The *Quran* testifies that a single act of charity is good enough to atone for many sins. Besides the routine charity, one is free to contribute more on other occasions, especially during Ramzan (*Sadaq*) which is considered as a great act of religious merit.

Haj: Mecca is revered as the most sacred place by the Muslims because it was built by Abraham, a Prophet and it is the birthplace of Muhammad, the last Prophet. Besides, it contains the sacred well Zamzam. At least once in a lifetime a Muslim should undertake the pilgrimage (*Haj*) to Mecca. Followers from all corners of the world undertake in Haj, and it is observed during the twelfth month of the Islamic calendar. *Haj* is obligatory for one who has fulfilled one's mundane duties, is physically healthy, economically solvent and can undertake it without harm or injury to the family members. While at Mecca, one has to perform certain rituals like moving around the *Kabah* seven times, every time kissing the black stone, hurling stones at the pillars at Mina which are construed as devil. A person should also engage in charity for the poor. One has to wear only two pieces of garments during *Haj*; one from navel to the knee, and the other covers the left shoulder and is tucked under the right. One should not wear shoes, but the use of sandals is permitted. On completing the tenth day one has to put off the prescribed robe (*Ihram*) and put on the normal clothes. Besides religious significance, the *Haj* has social significance too. It is a call for unity and universal brotherhood among the followers of Islam.

Jihad: Islam does not encourage passive tolerance of evil. It exhorts the faithful to remain in ever readiness to sacrifice anything and everything for the cause of Allah and the rule of righteousness on earth. The concept of '*Jihad*' has been more misunderstood than understood; it is not an act of violence against non-believers or non-conformists. Since everyone is created by God, the bond of brotherhood prevails among all men. No one is to be taken as a non-believer once and for all, since the Islamic fraternity is not a closed home. That is why the notion of freedom, self-effort, submission and grace of God remain significant for an individual till the state of highest good is attained. Islam, as a religion, began with induction of Khadija; and, later on grew into a world religion by expanding its embrace. Since the primary duty of an individual is to establish the rule of God on earth, it enjoins one to fight against all those forces that stand in the way. Use of force is to be essentially directed against those who are opposed to and are veritable barriers on the path of righteousness. When good and evil are pitted against each other one has to stand by the good and oppose the evil. But evil has to be checked and overcome by the use of force, only as the last choice and with the sole intention that it is being undertaken to establish the rule of God on earth, so that there is none who does not hear the message of God, there is none who is barred from following the path to Heaven and that the circumstances become germane so that everyone is out to believe and live the ways of God.

Besides *Quran*, Islamic ethics owes its justification to *Hadith* and *Saria*. *Hadith* contains teachings, in form of sayings, dialogues and the way Muhammad lived his life. The '*Shariah*' is a body of ethical injunctions with regard to the individual and social life; and, all social laws have to be in consonance with the '*Shariah*'. All social functions from the birth of a child, until one's burial are codified in the *Shariah*. There are injunctions: (1) which God commanded directly; and therefore are obligatory; (2) those that God recommended but did not make it obligatory; (3) those that God disapproved but did not prohibit in particular; (4) those that God prohibited and (5) those injunctions that God left undecided leaving it to the best judgment of the conscious believers and conscientious scholars. It contains guidelines pertaining to marriage, divorce, dowry, inheritance and funeral rites etc. Marriage is to be solemnized with the consent of the boy and girl and it is obligatory on the part of their interests. Polygamy is not forbidden; but, is permitted only under certain conditions. Similarly, lawful divorce is permitted only under certain conditions. Islam makes provision for stringent punishment for one whose conduct violates social ethics. Punishment has to be exemplary so that it serves as a deterrent against commissions of such mistakes by the others. Eve-teasers deserve whipping in the public. If a thief is caught red-handed, he deserves the punishment of his hands being chopped up. Virtues like service, humility, hospitality, brotherhood of man, obedience to parents are lauded. Sins like adultery, cheating, stealing, murder etc. are condemned.[8]

1.3.4. BUDDHISM

Buddhism was a reformation movement, and a reaction against the polytheism, ritualism and casteism of the Vedic tradition. Buddhism was averse to theoretical speculations and urged people to lead an ethical life, tempered with reason. It is an atheistic system. *Nirvāṇa* is the highest state which can be attained by self-effort i.e. without the aid of any super natural agency. It exhorts people to avoid extremes of self-indulgence on the one hand and self-abnegation on the other and follow the middle path (*majjhimā nikāya*), marked by practicality and reason. Buddha encouraged the followers to weigh his teachings against the touchstone of reason.

Buddha was born in the year 560 BC., to Suddhodana, the King of Sakya dynasty, who took every care, to keep Prince Siddhartha sequestered from sorrow, suffering, and the negativities of life. He was married to Princess Yashodhara and had a son-Rahul. But Siddhartha he was destined for something else. The sight of a sick man, a tottering old man and a corpse and a monk made him pensive, and ponder over the problem of suffering which every human-being is subject to. Eventually, he chose renunciation and became a recluse. His was the quest to find the panacea for human suffering. Therefore, he took to many preceptors and experimented with the life of rigorous penance and austerities. But these could not help him find the ultimate truths of life. Hence, he took to meditation under a banyan tree at Bodhagaya with the resolute determination, till enlightenment dawned upon him and Prince Siddhartha became the Buddha. Enlightenment marked another transition in his life when he decided to embrace life of a missionary in order to share the enlightenment with his fellowmen.

After the demise of Buddha, several attempts were made to codify the teachings of Buddha which finally took shape in the 3rd Council at Pataliputra in 241 BC. The *Tripiṭakas*: *Vinayapiṭaka*, *Suttapiṭaka*, and *Abhidhammapiṭaka*, are the holy books of Buddhism. The *Vinayapiṭaka* contains Buddha's teachings with regard to the rules of conduct for the monks, the *Suttapiṭaka* contains the principal doctrines which Buddha espoused, along with the dialogues and discourses of Buddha; and the *Abhidhammapiṭaka* contains philosophical doctrines.

Buddha maintained silence about all metaphysical questions, he was an agnostic. His silence with regard to ten fundamental questions has been variously interpreted. It would be appropriate to say that Buddha preferred to remain non-committal over uses and scholastic debates pertaining to God. He did not consider such philosophic discussions to be timely when the whole humanity is engulfed in suffering. *Nirvāṇa*, the highest state, can be attained by right knowledge, will and effort. Though Buddhism has no place for God, Buddha came to be worshipped later as God in Buddhist temples. *Bodhisattva* is one who is enlightened but defers his *Nirvāṇa*, and prefers to live in the world in order to help people attain *Nirvāṇa*. The Mahāyāna Buddhists even worship *Bodhisattvas*, the realized great souls who have attained enlightenment. Though the images of Buddha are found inside the temples, Buddha is worshipped more as the embodiment of compassion than as a Deity. Parallel to *Bodhisattva* in Mahāyāna Buddhism, *Arhats* are taken as realized persons by the followers of Hīnayāna.

Since God is not explicitly admitted, it is presumed that the world is eternal and self-sustained. Given the fact that there is the world, Buddhism articulates theories to explain the nature of the world and the dynamics of events therein. The doctrine of momentariness (*kṣaṇika vāda*) dwells upon the transitory nature of things in the world everything is momentary (*sarvam kṣaṇikam*) and nothing endures for more than a moment. A thing or a being is nothing but a series of changing states; for example, the so-called 'tree', is nothing but a tree-series. It is not the same tree at T_1, T_2, T_3, T_n (points of time). Hence, notions like 'singularity' or 'identity' do not reflect the true nature of Reality. The life of an individual is an aggregate of momentary states, because it is subject to mutation at every moment and this phenomenon of universal change is explained by the theory of dependent origination.

While emphasizing the momentariness of all phenomena, Buddhism underlines the universality of suffering. Ignorance is the primal cause of suffering because it is caused by attachment. Ignorance (*avidyā*) in the preceding life generates a disposition (*samskāra*) to be born again to fulfill the unfulfilled desires of the past. This result in consciousness in the embryo (*vijnāna*) which finds its expression in the birth of the individual, with body-mind complex (*nāma-rupa*) along with six organs of knowledge (*sadāyatanā*), which further leads to sense-object contact (*sparśa*), on account of which one has agreeable feelings (*vedanā*), the agreeable experience of the objects creates thrist (*tṛṣṇā*) for them and one clings to the world (*upādāna*), whereby, there is a tendency to be born again (*bhava*); this results in rebirth (*jati*) in future life, which is followed by old age and death (*jarā-marana*). This whole complex is what is known as the twelvefold chain of dependent origination (*bhavachakra*) in Buddhism.

An intriguing question in Buddhism is: How can it accept the concepts of rebirth, bondage, and liberation white declaring that there is no soul (*anatmavada)*? Who falls into bondage? What is that which attains liberation? The notion of bondage, rebirth and liberation presuppose the existence of soul. Contrary to the orthodox systems, which assume that the soul is an unchanging eternal substance, Buddhists advocate the thesis of no-soul (*anātmavāda*) which postulates that the Soul is an aggregate (*samghāta*). Human personality is a psycho-physical complex. It is an aggregate of matter (*rupa*), sensations (*vedanā*) perception (*samjnā*), tendency (*samskāra*) and consciousness (*vijnāna*). All the components constituting the whole (aggregate), is called personality. Similarly, the soul is nothing but the configuration of the five components. Buddhists contend that there is rebirth even though there is nothing to be reborn. There is rebirth in the sense of continuity of life-series. Birth and death are points of transition in the life cycle. The last moment of the series called 'past' (life) is followed by the first moment of series called the 'present' (life) and the last moment of the series called the 'present' shall be followed by the first moment of series called 'future'. The cycle goes on, until one escapes to a vantage point where one remains immune to the dynamics of life cycle. It is known as the state of *Nirvāna*.[9]

Misery and suffering are facts of life, Suffering has a cause if, the cause is removed, the effect gets negated thereby resulting *Nirvāna*. *Nirvāna* literally means "state of extinction", Nirvana is an existential state which can be attained here and now, exemplified in the life of Buddha. On attaining *Nirvāna,* one escapes the cycle of transmigration (*bhavachakra*) and related sufferings, thereby. It is not merely a negative state, characterized by absence of pain and misery but a state of positive, contentment and bliss. *Nirvāna* does not mean negation of existence but points to a state of existence where there is neither the commotion of desires nor the rule of passions. There is no scope for rebirth because there is no desire for anything whatsoever. There is no desire because the individual does not have the sense of clinging. Due to right knowledge, one learns the art of living in the world without belonging to it. It urges one to live a life of love, compassion, non-attachment and service. It inspires one to embrace a life of activism, explicitly exemplified in the missionary life of Buddha. *Nirvāṇa* can be attained by perseverance only, without the mediation of any supernatural agency. It is a creed of self-help. Buddha exhorts his followers, "Be a lamp unto thyself".

"*Nirvāṇa* is profound like an ocean, lofty like a mountain peak. *Nirvāṇa* is not past nor future, nor present nor produced nor not produced nor producible".

Buddha begins with a note of realism in pointing out that suffering is universal and that it is due to worldly attachment to phenomena resulting from ignorance. This blinds one to the truth that all objects of enjoyment are transitory. When one comes to realize the impermanence (momentariness of things), passions give way to detachment and renunciation. Buddha did not rest content in indicating the possibility of *Nirvāṇa* but elaborated practical ways by which everyone, irrespective of caste, colour and creed can attain it.

One can attain perfection become, an *Arhat* through right conduct (*śila*), concentration (*samādhi*) and knowledge (*prajñā*), these constitute the three pillrs of Buddhist ethics. The eight fold path enjoined by Buddha is the Middle Path. They are: right view (*samyag dṛsti*), right resolve (*samyag saṅkalpa*), right speech (*samyag vāk*), right conduct (*samyag karmānta*), right livelihood (*samyag jiva*), right effort (*samyag vyāyāma*), right mindfulness (*samyag smṛti*) and right concentration (*samyag samādhi*). Right view is cultivated through proper understanding of the four noble truths; namely: (a) suffering is universal (*sarvam duḥkham*), (b) there is cause of suffering (*duḥkha samudāya*) (c) Cessation of suffering (*duḥkha nirodha*) and (d) practical ways of attaining it (*duḥkh nirodha mārga*) i.e. the (*astānga mārga*). The thought and utterance of threefold submission (*śaraṇas*) constitute the core of Buddhist ethics. They are: *Buddham śaraṇam gachhāmi*, *Dhammam śaraṇam gachhāmi* and *Saṅgham śaraṇam gachhāmi*. Buddha is the ultimate ideal as he embodies *Dhamma*, is the ultimate Truth, the knowledge of which liberates one from the cycle of birth and death. "*Saṅgha*" points to the need of organized effort which facilitates one's effort to attain *Nirvāṇa*. *Pancaśīla* outlines the core ethical principles of Buddhism i.e. (a) Do not kill (b) Do not steal (c) Do not lie (d) Do not take to intoxication and, (e) Do not commit adultery.

The *Hīnayāna* and the *Mahāyāna* are the two principal sects of Buddhism. The followers of Hinayana are orthodox and puritanical, and they follow the scripture in letter and spirit. On the other hand, the followers of *Mahāyāna* are more progressive and accommodative. The *summum bonum* of *Hīnayāna* is the attainment of Arhathood, whereas that of *Mahāyāna* is the state of Bodhisattva. The former characterises the highest state as complete dissolution of ego through removal of the veil of passions and cravings (*kleśāvaraṇa*), whereas *Mahāyāna*, emphasizes the further necessity for removing the veil of ignorance which shrouds knowledge (*jnāna*) by means of dialectics. *Hīnayāna* cult has lesser following and is practiced mostly in the Southern parts, Ceylon, South India and Burma. *Mahāyāna* (Greater Vehicle) has larger following in The Northern areas Tibet, China, Thailand and Japan. *Hīnayāna* keeps itself strictly away from worship and rituals whereas theistic practices involving rites and rituals gradually crept into *Mahāyāna* Buddhism.[10]

1.3.5. JUDAISM

Judaism, the religion of the Hebrews is based on the revelations of God (Jehovah) to Prophet Moses on Mount Sinai. Prophet Abraham is taken as the first Prophet whom God chose to lead the people and promised that his successors would multiply. Old Testament, the holy book of the Jews contains three distinct parts, namely; *Laws*, *Prophets* and *Writings*. The *Laws* contain the revelation of God to Prophet Moses. *Torah*, the book of ethics, consists of 613 basic precepts and it provides exhaustive guidance to live one's life. The *Prophets* consists of the historical records which depict the enactments and sayings of the great *Prophets* who came after Moses. The Writings contain cryptic ethical injunctions, Psalms and Proverbs (wisdom literature).

Judaism is strictly monotheistic - God is one, without a second and is represented by Yāhweh. He is the creator of the cosmos and is omnipotent and omniscient. As transcendent, He is beyond human comprehension. Hence, all human descriptions of Him are analogical or metaphorical. As the omnipotent, He is unlimited, and can will anything into existence, as He created the world out of his divine fiat, *ex nihilo*.

Man is privileged to be the best creation of God because God created human beings in His image, and entrusted them with dominion over all beings. God's essential nature is disclosed only through His revelations to the Prophets and His enactments, in human history from time to time. God declared the Jews as His chosen people. Abraham, the ancestor of the Jews had the first covenant with God. The history of Judaism is the history of God's fellowship with the chosen people of Israel. Judaism does not give much credence to philosophical speculations because God and His ways fall beyond the ambit of reason. This does not undermine reason, but yield its dividends as long as a person remains subservient to faith as codified in the Book of Law (*Torah*). God, the supreme Father, loves one and all and as the sovereign, He metes out punishment to the wrong-doers i.e. those who disobey His commandments. He forgives the penitent sinner; irrespective of how great the sins are. This exemplifies His merciful nature as well as His role as a benefactor and that of a strict disciplinarian. Since He is just and righteous, anyone who follows the path of righteousness wins His love. Judaism stresses fellowship with God in the form of 'I-Thou' encounter.

The forces of nature follow their course as per the will of God which explains why the world presents a grand orderliness and design. Though there is a belief in the after - world, the world that one lives in is of paramount importance because it is the working ground that helps one cultivate love for God, it is also a place to work out one's excellence by making the momentous choice between right and wrong.

There are two factions in Judaism: (1) The PHARISEES accepted the existence of Angels, and the Resurrection of the body. (Acts 23:8) and (2) the SADDUCEES denied both (Mt. 22:23) (Acts 23:8) accepts the reality of angels and devils that represent 'good' and 'evil' respectively. They believe in the immortality of the soul which outlives the body on physical death which is bound up with the notion of the Day of Judgment when one stands accountable for one's deeds, good and bad. The Jews believe that soul is that into whose nostrils God breathed at the time of birth. And death means passing out of the breath. A Hebrew believes in a three tiered universe i.e. Heaven (abode of God), Earth (abode of human beings) and Sheol (abode of the dead). They alone believe in the resurrection of the dead on the Day of Judgment.

They strongly believe in the advent of the Messiah who will come in human form to secure salvation for all Jews and establish a kingdom of universal love, peace and harmony when all heterogeneities and differences shall sink and a time shall come when the lion and lamb shall drink from the same fountain.

God created man in the likeness of Him. So human beings are uniquely privileged with freewill and are entrusted with the role of being the custodian of other living phenomena. Since human beings are essentially spiritual one's foremost duty is to observe the moral law enjoined in the *Torah*. (wo)man has to live as a faithful servant of God and try one's best to translate His will for establish his rule on earth. Since man is uniquely endowed with freewill, one may commit sin as well, but sin is forgiven when there is genuine repentance on the part of the individual. Judaism leaves no room for asceticism or renunciation as it exhorts the believers to live a life of love and righteousness. Though the world is not eternal, a person's can attain eternity because of one's spiritual nature and one's righteous deeds. A person's final destiny is to attain membership of Heaven where one lives in eternal fellowship with God and angels, where there is no physical body. One lives there in one's spiritual nature along with the world of spirits, which is bereft of eating, drinking, procreation, greed, and jealousy etc., nothing of the kind which characterizes bodily existence.

If a person does not follow the commandments of God, one comes to realize their significance while paying the price for such disobedience. Disobeying the commandments does not mean slavery or scant regard for the demands of reason but it is improper use of 'reason' because real freedom involves making reason subservient to the will of God. An ideal human life is one which is tempered with justice, love, mercy, humility, readiness to repent for one's sins and invoking God's forgiveness. Since human beings are the crown of creation, God blessed them to be fruitful and multiply so that they can translate the divine purpose in the world. (Wo)man is prone to sin but one is endowed with the capacity to introspect and repent for one's follies; sincere penitence and intense prayer take a person closer to the Father.

Suffering is of great significance in the *Weltanschauung* of the Jews. The history of the Jews is a saga of suffering and persecution. In 590 BC they had to suffer exile in Babylonia, and court confinement for one hundred fifty years. Subsequently, their temple was demolished in 78 AD; millions suffered the atrocities of Auschwitz. For a Jew, suffering is vicarious, Israel as a nation, feels that they are the chosen people of God. So, they vindicate the glory of God by living in accordance with His commandments and treat themselves as people ready to suffer for the cause of God and find positive design behind prolonged suffering of their community. They view suffering either as the result of their past sin or as part of God's design to prepare them as fit instruments to translate His will. It is only through suffering that they can work out their own redemption and that of the rest of the human kind. They construe history as precious because the memories of the past have a chastening influence on the individual as well as the collective mind which makes them fit to receive the future revelations of God, from time to time in future. Though God lets humanity to suffer, He remains vigilant and protective so that humanity is saved, for e.g., the great flood summoned by God, was to punish human beings for their sin, but did not efface human kind from the surface of the earth because of His protective love.

Suffering is not an evil (but is necessary) because it corrects the wrong doer and purifies one who undergoes the suffering with love and gratitude; as is exemplified in the life of Abraham, Joseph and Job. Sometimes the phenomenon of unmerited suffering i.e. the suffering of the truthful, just and innocent, appear to be intriguing which human mind fails to comprehend. Hence, the Jews resign completely with the conviction that nothing can take place without God's will or loving dispensation, as He is the ultimate arbiter. The Jews view such suffering as having a place in the great design of things.

Judaism demands strict conformity to the Ten Commandments. (a) Thou shalt have no gods before me. (b) Thou shalt not make unto the in graven image. (c) Thou shalt not take the name of the Lord, thy God in vain (d) Remember Sabbath day to keep it holy. (e) Honour thy father and thy mother (f) Thou shalt not kill. (g) Thou shalt not commit adultery. (h) Thou shalt not steal. (i) Thou shalt not bear false witness against thy neighbor. (k) And thou shalt not covet thy neighbor's housewife, maid servant, ox, ass etc. There are six forms of services which has to be performed, provide clothes to the unclad, nurse the sick, comfort the mourners, bury the dead, stay away from vanity and vices like lying, maneuvering, giving false witness, killing the innocent, hypocrisy and usury.

Fervent prayer bridges the chasm between man and God. It is obligatory to pray three times a day in the morning, noon and evening. One can pray by oneself or in an assembly. Congregational prayers are conducted in the Synagogue where passages are read from the Hebrew Scripture. There are certain rites for prayer, both the feet are to remain as close as possible, with eyes closed, head hung forward and hands placed on the heart at the time of prayer. If one prays by looking at the book, the eyes should not be taken off. While in Israel, one should face Jerusalem; but, while praying outside Israel, one should face towards the homeland (Israel). Prayer is an opportunity when a believer shares one's desires and grievances with God, the Lord. Marriage is a sacrament, neither a contract nor a convenience. It is obligatory for every male, even a slave, to undergo circumcision on the eighth day after birth (LK 2:21) (GEN 17: 10-14)

The Jews observe Saturday as the 'Sabbath day', the Holy Day. Besides, there are some principal festivals in a year. The festival of Passover is observed in the month of Abibe commemorating the time (month) when they left for their own land from Egypt. This marks the liberation of Jews from prolonged slavery. The 'Harvest Festival' is observed to mark the harvesting of crops and the "Festival of Shelters" is celebrated in the month of autumn when people gather fruits from vineyards and orchards. The New Year witnesses gala celebration by the Jews which marks the beginning of the history of the Jewish race, reminding them of God's creation. Moreover, a particular day is earmarked for collective atonement when it is mandatory for the believers to congregate in the Synagogue to repent for their sins or acts of moral turpitude.

Judaism is divided into two broad sects namely: the Orthodox and the Progressive. The orthodox demand non-compromising obedience to the laws laid down by Moses and those enjoined in the *Talmud* (ethical treatise) which came to be compiled by the Rabbis. They are, by and large, given to ostentatious practices and priestly injunctions. On the other hand, the Progressive sect underlines the importance of following the cardinal moral tenets and living the life of rectitude. In other words, the Orthodox sect follows the tradition in letter, whereas the Progressive sect follows the spirit of their holy books, leaving room for change and adaptability, in keeping with demands of time. [11]

CHAPTER - 2

ARGUMENTS FOR THE EXISTENCE OF GOD

God occupies Centre-stage in most of the religions. Though God doesn't have explicit place in the non-theistic religion, state of Godhood, perfection is taken as ultimate goal of life. God is conceived differently as the 'first cause', 'intelligent principle', 'absolute world ground', 'most perfect being conceivable' and culmination of human strivings. God is spontaneously postulated as supremely real. But human mind looks for reasons and justifications for this. Is God a subjective necessity of the religiosity actuated minds? Are there reasons which shall coerce one to accept God as a valid article of knowledge by everyone? There have been manifold attempts to articulate the arguments in favour of 'existence of God'.[1]

2.1. COSMOLOGICAL ARGUMENT

Cosmological argument derived from the Greek terms cosmos (world or Universe) and logos (reason or rational account). The common theme among them all is that there is cosmos which exists, rather than just nothing, it must have been caused by something beyond it.[2] Cosmological argument is a-*posteriori* in so far as it seeks to prove the existence of God from the act of existence of the cosmos. It is also termed as causal argument because it postulates God as the uncaused cause of the world-effect. The argument takes two forms. Either it appeals to 'law of causality' or 'contingency of the world'. In the former, God is posited as the primordial cause and in the latter; God is construed as the absolute ground of the contingent world.

Argument as first formulated by Saint Anselm in 11th century. He argues that everything that exists is brought about either by something or comes out of nothing. The second possibility is ruled out because nothing can beget only nothing. So, whatever exists, exists on account of something.

Everything in the universe requires something through which it comes into its existence or that it exists through no medium. Since it is impossible for nothing to come out of nothing (*ex nihilio nihil fit*) whatever then already exists only exists through something.[3]

In order to explain the existence of a thing, the existence of the 'other' is admitted. The 'other' may be either one or more than one. If there is more than one, then there are three possibilities, (a) the world of particulars owe their existence to one thing through which they come to exists, (b) each one of them exists through itself, i.e. there is plurality of independent others, (c) particulars owe their existence to one, it would eventually point to a singular, primordial 'other' which is God. If each exists through its capacity for self-existence then each thing must eventually owe its existence to a single power. In such case, everything would owe its existence to one power i.e. God, through whom they come to possess the capacity to exist. Plurality of independent others violates the canons of reason. It is logically odd to suppose that there is more than one thing through which everything comes into existence. If things owe their existence to one another, then the world as a whole would owe its explanation to something beyond itself. Therefore everything that exists, exists through this one thing by which all else comes into existence. This one thing trough which all these other finite things exist is thus beyond them. That through which everything else exists must be real and more real than everything else.

"Therefore, that which exists through itself most of all..... This is necessarily supremely good, supremely great and is of all things that exist, the Supreme. Therefore, there is something which, whether it is called an essence, a substance or a nature, is the best and the greatest and of all the things that is the Supreme".

According to Descartes idea of 'God' as an absolutely perfect being is innate. Innate ideas are different from adventitious ideas, produced by the external objects and fictitious ideas, constructed by human mind. The argument in favour of the existence of God takes two different forms. He wishes to establish the existence of God from the concept of God and proceeds to prove the reality of God from deriving the reality of his own existence.

For every effect there is a cause and the cause must at least have as much reality as the effect. Hypothetically, if effect possesses more reality than the cause, it would mean that the extra reality that the effect possesses was produced out of nothing. This is a patent violation of the logical principle, *exnihilo nihilo fit.*

There must be as much reality in the efficient and total cause as in its effect, for everything that is derives its existence from something which already contains it as the seed contains the tree that evolves out of it.[4]

This is true not only of facts but also of ideas. Our minds conceive of an infinite perfect being (God) at the same time of finite imperfect creatures. According to the principle of causality, the idea of God must have had a cause and the cause must have been at least as much real as the effect. He argues 'I' (individual) could not have been the cause of the idea of the infinite and perfect being for the simple reason that myself, being finite and imperfect, could not have been the cause of the idea of 'infinite' and 'perfection'. For the same reason, no finite being other than myself could have been the cause of this idea in me. Reason demands that the cause of such idea must not have been less real than something which is infinite and perfect itself. Hence, one is logically led to conclude that the idea of 'Infinite' and perfection must have been implanted in my mind by a reality which is infinite and perfect.

While advancing the arguments, Descartes guards against two possibilities, namely. 'Infinite is negation of the 'finite' and that the term 'Infinite' doesn't mean actual 'Infinite' but potential 'Infinite'. If the first possibility is conceded to, then 'infinite' need not be really existent. In such case, it becomes a mere idea which one gets by merely thinking (imagining) that 'Infinite' is not like the finites which are experienced. Descartes argues that the idea of infinite, far from being a negative idea, is the most primitive and positive of all ideas. Rather, 'finite' derives its meaning from the idea of 'infinite'. We have already had the idea of 'perfection' in us in relation to which we construe ourselves and other things as finite and imperfect. If the second possibility is acknowledged, then 'mind' can be conceived as potentially infinite, though not actually infinite. Then, there is no oddity in thinking that 'mind' contains all the perfections that are ascribed to God in potential form. So, there is no anomaly in thinking that mind is the cause of the idea of God could not have been produced by 'mind' which is potentially perfect. A potential perfect mind cannot produce the idea of an actual perfect being i.e. God. Hence, God must actually exist to produce the idea of a being that is perfect and infinite.

He then proceeds to establish the fact of God's existence from his own. He argues, "I cannot be the cause of my own existence because in that case, I would have been complete and there would not have been any desire at all. Perfection would not be acting in me. But, I am utterly conscious of my dependence on others. My parents could not have been the cause of my existence though I owe them my body and psychological dispositions. But the fact that, I possess the idea of a 'perfect being' rules out this possibility because my parents who are as imperfect as myself, could not have been the cause of this idea any more than myself. Since a cause must possess as much reality as the effect, nothing other than God could have given me the idea of perfection against which I consider myself imperfect." He rules out the possibility of several causes producing the idea of several qualities which we attribute to God, so that there are different agents (cause) producing different ideas like 'infinite' 'perfection', 'omnipotence' etc. it is argued that the idea of 'Infinite being' contains the unity of all perfections, absent in individual agent.

Unity, the simplicity or inseparability of all the properties of the oddity is one of the chief perfections I conceive him to possess and the idea of this unity of all the perfections of Deity could certainly not be put into my mind by any cause from which I did not like wise receive the idea of all other perfections for no power could enable me to think of an inseparable unity without at the same time giving me the knowledge of what they were.

Leibnitz underlines the fact of unity of the universe. 'Unity' reveals the characteristic nature of reality. For everything that exists, there must be sufficient reason as to why it is as it is and why does it exist at all, rather than not being there. The reason for the existence of a 'particular' is to be found in its cause and the reason of the cause is to be found in the preceding cause and so on. Thus, in order to find sufficient reason for particular things one has to go back in the causal series. But howsoever one goes back in the causal series. But however one goes back in the causal series one shall never find a state which contains sufficient reasons as to why there should be a world at all, rather than there being nothing at all and why should the world be such, as it is. Even if it is conceded that there is an eternal succession of states, there must be reason as to why at all there are things that succeed one another. Even if one explains the existence of individual things, one can hardly explain the fact of unity in the procession of things and events. The explanation of unity as well as sufficient reason of the world, is to be found in the extra mundane entity i.e. God. Reason of the world lies in 'extra mundane' which doesn't belong to the successive chain of states.

The reasons of the world then lie in something extra mundane, different from the chain of states or series of things whose aggregate constitute the world and so we pass from physical or hypothetical necessity which determines the subsequent things of world by the earlier to something which is the absolute or metaphysical necessity for which no reason can be given. J.L. Mackie directs his polemics against the cosmological argument which seeks to prove the existence of God as the sole ground of the world which is contingent. He questions the principle of sufficient reason which runs as follows, "as nothing can occur without sufficient reason there must be sufficient reason for the world as a whole". He asks; why should it be supposed that everything must have a sufficient reason? Why should one presume that there is a being which contains sufficient explanation of its own existence?

Cosmological arguments constitute the second in the series of five arguments, adduced by Thomas Aquinas. Everything that exists owes its being to the activity of some other thing which is its cause. Again, that which is a cause in relation to its effect, owes its proceeds back in the causal series, one has to arrive at a point which is not only the first member of the series but is self-caused. So, there must be the first cause of everything which is it uncaused. The argument draws its strength from the assumption that 'infinite regress' is a logical fallacy. If infinite regress is admitted one cannot find a conclusive explanation for any existent whatsoever. If the thing 'A' , owes its explanation to 'B' which is the cause or part of the cause of 'A' and 'B', in turn, is caused by 'C', it simply means that if 'B' were not present, then 'A' would not have been there and if 'C' were not there, then neither 'B' nor 'A' could have been there. Those who deny the first cause let us suppose 'X', would thereby deny the existence of everything that exists. Thus, the thesis of 'infinite series' is an absurdity. So, a first cause must have been there, which is God.[5]

The basis of the cosmological argument is that the universe cannot account for its own existence. Why do things exist at all? Why is there something rather than nothing? There must be a reason, the argument says, for the existence of the Universe, and this reason has to be something which is not part of the physical world of time and space. This argument has a very long history. Plato, in *Timaeus*, argument that everything must have been created by some cause. Aristotle argued that behind the series of cause and effect in the world there must be an Uncaused Mover, and the Kalam argument in Islam is an attempt to show that the universe must have a cause and is not the result of an infinite regress (an endless chain going back for ever). Cosmological questions that arise are "what is the purpose of something existing rather than nothing? What is the reason behind the universe's existence? The conclusion drawn from these questions is that since everything has a cause the cause of off causes is the causeless which is God.

A third form of cosmological argument is referred to as the kalam argument – the term 'kalam' being an Arabic word meaning 'speculative theology.'[6] It was originally articulated by medieval Arabic philosophers and subsequently developed by William Craig and J.P. Moreland. 'Kalam' is derived from the word 'cosmos' which means the created universe. The argument is developed in form of a dilemma. The phenomenal universe either had a beginning or always existed and was beginning less. If there was a beginning, the beginning was caused by something or was not caused by anything. If the beginning was the effect of a cause, then that cause was either a personal entity or an impersonal force. The argument seeks to prove that the universe had a beginning and that it was caused by a personal entity.

The thesis that universe had a beginning precludes the possibility of infinite series. Here, distinction is drawn between 'potential infinite' and 'actual infinite'. The concept of 'potential infinite' is logically untenable. Potential infinite is that which is actually 'finite' but has the potentiality to grow into 'infinite'. But there is no point of time when the potential infinite can be said to have realized its infinitude. A potentially infinite series goes on increasing by addition of numbers but a time shall never come when it becomes an actual infinite. Hence, a potential infinite, in principle, remains always a finite. In this sense, a potential infinite remains a hypothetical construct and can hardly contain explanation of the real existence of finites. Similarly, thesis of 'actual infinite' doesn't stand to reason. Since a temporal series that is beginning less cannot exist an actual infinite cannot therefore be said to exist. The thesis of 'actual infinite' gives rise to logically unacceptable consequences. Craig illustrates this in asking one to imagine that there is a library with infinite number of books and then to suppose that here are infinite number of red books and infinite number of black books as well. Does it not imply that there are as many black books in the library as there are red books? Hypothetically, if black books are taken away, then the entire amount of books in the library shall remain the same as before since the library has an infinite number of books. Consequently, the stock of books in the library shall remain always infinite, irrespective of the books issued to readers or damaged otherwise. It is logically impossible, therefore, technically and empirically impossible to traverse actual infinite series, either forward by successive addition or backward, by subtraction. It is impossible to count 'infinite' because there shall always be a number to succeed at a given point of time. 'Actual infinite' remains unattainable, in principle. It is absurd to think of a beginning less, temporal series. unless a first point of series is presumed to have really occurred, the succeeding moment could not have come into existence and down in the series, 'the present' which is real, could not have been real (actual). Unless the past is assumed to have been a summation of finite series, the moment called 'present' could not have been real. In this sense, the 'past' means the time span between the first point of the series and the moment, called the 'present'.

Cosmological argument takes a different form in the hands of Herbert McCabe. He argues that the question pertaining to the existence of god cannot be logically avoided because the world, as a whole, demands an explanation in terms of a trans-mundane or trans-physical. The 'why' question, meaningfully raised with regard to certain particulars, can also be asked about certain fundamental questions about the world. Certain features of the world which otherwise remain unexplainable, demand a God-centric ontology for their explanation. Not to entertain questions about the world as a whole, simply because they don't have answers, satisfying our scientific temper, is simply to beg the question. A real atheist is one who rests contented in asking questions within the world but fails to see that the world itself raises a question which needs to be answered with urgency. It is noteworthy that the 'why' questions or 'how' questions can be raised at different levels of generality. He argues that how come a particular dog say, 'Fido', is answered in pointing to the mother dog and the question 'why' of a particular species takes us to greater degree of generality. Here, one may be forced to reflect on the 'dog species' as a whole. The same question 'How come Fido? May also mean how did this dog as a living species come into being. A satisfactory answer to this question shall make us reflect upon the origin of species in general and dog species, in particular. One cannot answer this question without appealing to laws of physics, biochemistry and comparative anatomy by way of tracing the evolution of species *vis*-a-*vis* the existence of the material world.

If explanation of the universe is to be provided through the God-hypothesis, then God, obviously cannot be taken as an inhabitant of universe. So, the question why? and how come? Which can be meaningfully raised in respect of a particular, cannot be raised in respect of God. McCabe urges us to be on guard so that one does not smuggle anything extra to the concept of God. The claim that universe is dependent on God does not tell us anything additional about the character of the universe. Since all our knowledge about the God is derived from what we know about the universe, how can we come back from God with additional information about the world?

We do not appeal specifically to God to explain why the universe is this way rather that. For this we need only appeal to explanations within the universe. What God account is that the universe is there, instead of nothing?[7]

2.2. ONTOLOGICAL ARGUMENT

Ontological argument derived from the Greek terms *ontos* (being) and logos (rational account). The ontological argument, first developed by Saint Anselm of Canterbury, takes a variety of forms.[8] Ontological argument is a-priori in character. It seeks to deduce the existence of god from the concept 'God'. The coinage of the term is ascribed to Immanuel Kant. But the argument was first formulated by Saint Anselm in 11th century. According to this argument, from the analysis of the concept 'God', one can conclude that 'god necessarily exists'. It permits logical passage from the concept 'God' to the existence of god. In other words, one who has an adequate understanding of 'God', knows that 'God exists'. Unlike existence of other finites which exist contingently, God exists necessarily. Conversely, for one who understands 'what is God', the statement that 'God doesn't exist' is an absurdity. The argument takes the form of *reductio ad absurdum*. Since one cannot conceive of God which doesn't exist, God must be one that necessarily exists whereas in case of other particulars one can think of their non-existence.

"God cannot be conceived not to exist… God is that than which nothing greater can be conceived."

If God is that than which nothing greater can be conceived', it follows that He cannot exist in the mind only because that which exists in the mind as a mere idea, is less real than the one which exists in the mind (as an idea) as well in reality, outside mind.

The strength of the argument rests on the expression, 'nothing greater can be conceived'. The term 'greater' is here used qualitatively to signify perfection. The expression, 'than which nothing greater can be conceived', means that God is the greatest or the most perfect being that can ever be conceived. God must exist because the non-existence of Him would imply imperfection, for one can think of an entity which not only exists in the mind but also as a matter of fact. The argument obviously assumes that 'existence' as property is integral to the notion of perfection whereas 'non-existence' as a property is the mark of imperfection. God must necessarily exist for He would otherwise cease to be what He is. Thus, the statement 'God necessarily exists' follows from the notion of God. On the contrary, the non-existence of God is incompatible with the idea of God. As one cannot understand fire without its thermal properly, one cannot think of God who is non-existence.

Gaunilo advances objections against Anselm's formulation of the argument. From the fact that, we have notion of something, it doesn't follow that there is a reality corresponding to it. For example, from the idea of a perfect island (meaning that than which nothing greater can be conceived), nothing follows about the real existence of such an island. According to Gaulino, Anselm's argument is the result of confusion between the concept of something and its existence in reality. If Anselm's view is conceded to then one would not know how to differentiate between mere concepts in mind and the concepts that have instantiation in the world. Anselm replies that there is clear distinction between the notion of the "most perfect island" and that "than which nothing greater can be thought". While talking about God, one is concerned with the latter. There is no oddity in maintaining that the most perfect island conceived by mind, is not available in the world. But unlike this, God's perfection subsumes the idea of necessary existence. To think of "God" than which nothing greater can be conceived, is to think of something which means that it is without a beginning. Something which has no beginning cannot be thought as a non-existent. That which did not exist can be thought of as beginning to exist. Aquinas, the medieval thinker, argues that meaningfulness of the concept of God does not entail any conclusion about its existence, even though there is a sense in which the non-existence of god is unthinkable. To entertain the idea of god is to have the idea of existence but from this it does not follow that such a Being exists, as a matter fact.

Ontological argument is reformulated by Descartes. He argues that the idea is innate. An adventitious idea is that which is produced by the mind by external objects for example, a real lake produces the idea of lake in the mind. Fictitious idea is that which is concocted by the mind out of the adventitious ideas. Unlike the two kinds of ideas, the idea of God is innate. It is neither produced in the mind by anything in the world nor is it a figment of imagination. It is integral to human thinking. Innateness of the idea of God means that people are inherently disposed to have the idea of God without any prior experience of him in reality. Whenever one entertains the idea of God, one necessarily thinks of a supremely perfect Being i.e. a being who possesses all perfections, actual or possible. Existence is a part of perfection. So, a perfect Being cannot be thought of as non-existence in reality. So, God exists. As one cannot separate the idea of a triangle from the fact that 'its three angles are equal to two right angles', it is not possible to think of a supremely perfect Being (God) who lacks existence.

Objections against ontological argument are more explicitly articulated by Kant. He submits that existence is not a property. To say that 'X exists doesn't add anything to our knowledge or definition of X'. It simply means that 'X', along with its essential properties, is an object of experience. There is no contradiction in saying that 'X' with its essential qualities, is not available in the world as there is no absurdity in thinking of 'X' as non-saying that god, with all the qualities of perfection, doesn't exist. One can't define things into existence. Though, in the level of thought one cannot separate an idea from its essential characteristics, there is no oddity in thinking that there is no corresponding existence in reality.

Gassendi opines that 'real existence' cannot form a part of the idea of perfection. Existence is that on account of which a thing in question (here God) would exist along with its perfection. It is fallacious to say that 'existence' as a quality, resides in a thing in the manner in which other perfections do. One is free to think of a horse with wings without thinking of its existence, which, of course, might be considered as greater perfection, if it were really present. Similarly, one is free to think of God having omniscience, omnipotence, omnipresence and other perfections without thinking of Him as existing (in fact) along with all these perfections. Contrarily, if the idea of god as a supremely perfect Being can be said to exist, the idea of a perfect Pegasus (having perfection as one of its qualities) can be said to co-exist with God. Descartes replies to Gassendi in pointing out that one should be on guard in taking 'existence', as a property, like omnipotence. Property is that which can be predicated of a thing. But necessary existence, as a property, can be predicated of God alone. Unlike other things, 'necessary existence' forms part of God's 'essence'. The existence of a triangle should not be compared with the existence of god because the relationship between 'existence' and 'essence' is radically different in case of God. In the expression 'God is existent' the 'is' is not a new predicate but serves as a copula which brings the predicate in relation to the subject. It does not enrich our conception of the subject as a 'predicate' does. So, the expression 'there is God' does not yield any new information about God. It simply says that the God along with all its predicates exists. The idea of 100 dollars does not ensure that there are really 100 dollars in my pocket.

Frege and Russel argue that 'existence' is not a real predicate. One can understand a statement without being sure that there are particular instances of it in reality, with properties satisfying the description in the statement. 'Existence-statement' is, therefore, logically different from 'existence things'. One does not know a thing when one learns that it exists. In other words, 'existence' as a property, doesn't enter into the account of what something is.

In the same breath, Caters argues; even if it is granted that a supremely perfect Being carries the implication of necessary existence by virtue of its very title, it doesn't follow from this that the 'existence', in question, is anything actual in the world. All that it means is that the idea of 'necessary existence' is inseparably linked with the concept of 'supremely perfect

Being'. One cannot infer that 'God exists' from the idea of 'God' unless it is otherwise supposed that a supreme being actually exists.

Malcom holds that if God exists at all, His existence is necessary because God could not have been caused to come into existence by some other entity. Either God exists or doesn't exist. If He did not exist, His existence would have been impossible because He cannot be made to come into existence by any extraneous agent. If He does exist, He obviously doesn't owe it to any other factor nor is His existence, contingent. If He is said to exists, He cannot stop exist. So, God's existence is either impossible or necessary.

"If God a Being greater than which cannot be conceived, doesn't exist then he cannot come into existence. For if He did He would either have been caused to come into existence or have happened to come into existence and in either case. He would be a limited Being, which according to our conception of God is not the case. Hence if God exists, His existence becomes necessary. Thus, God's existence is either impossible or necessary."[9]

2.3. TELEOLOGICAL ARGUMENT

As seen in the previous chapter, from the cosmological questions raised before therein we concluded that the universe had a beginning and a creator responsible for it. On the other hand teleological arguments begin with certain aspects of the world and conclude that there is a grand designer who is the cause of the world and has mental properties such as intention, knowledge and purpose.[10]

The portents of teleological argument invoke the existence of God so as to account for certain aspects of the world. The universe is of the nature of a grand design, a marvellous labyrinth. Therefore, it could not have been brought into existence by mere chance or accident nor could it create itself. In other words, the way the world functions i.e. things and events in the state of nature behave; do necessarily presuppose that there is an intelligent author of the cosmos. Things do not take place at random. They do occur with precision, regularity and are found to converge to one 'end'. Design arguments draw their strength from the fact of regularity and the notion of 'end' which things and events do tend to achieve. Knowledge of regularities help man manipulates nature and makes predictions possible. Knowledge is power. Given the fact of regularities, scientists explain them through causal dynamics. But they can hardly explain why at all there are uniformities rather than there being random or chance occurrences. Given the uniformities, the evolutionists seek to explain change, progress and retardation in the state of nature. In other words, their focus is to account for the survival and growth of the species rather than their arrival or origin. The design argument is cast in the analogy of creation of human artefact.

Plato argues that regularity, motion and the cosmos as a whole, is the work of the divine craftsmen (demi-urge). Thomas Aquinas marshals his argument by appealing to 'end' rather than to the regularities. Everything in the state of nature is found to move towards one end. In production of things, 'final cause' (end) is more important than the material and efficient cause. Material and efficient cause can, at most, explain the origin of certain effects but they can hardly explain the perceived harmony and orderliness, converging to certain end. If things would happen accidentally then harmony and purposiveness would remain the perpetual enigma. They cannot be attributed to chance because things which happen by chance only happen rarely. If an arrow moves in a particular direction and hits a target, then one can legitimately infer that the archer, who shot the arrow, had a target in view. If things in the state of nature are found to converge to one end then it must have been the result planning on the part of a supremely intelligent entity God. As nature lacks awareness and intelligence, it cannot direct itself to a goal.

"Nothing… that lacks awareness tends to a goal except under the direction of someone with awareness and with understanding. The arrow, for example, requires an archer. Everything in nature, therefore, is directed to its goal by someone with understanding, this we call God."

William Paley tries to fortify design argument by the analogy of watch and the watchmaker. While passing through a health, if one stumbles against a big piece of stone, its solitary presence can be attributed to a heavy gust of wind. But if, per chance, one comes across a watch it cannot be attributed to chance. It would be height of absurdity to suppose that the watch has been there on account of the chance assembling of the minute parts. It is improbable that springs, wheels, pins came together accidentally leading to synchronic movement of them, as a result of which the watch records time with precision. One has to admit the reality of a watchmaker to account for the presence of a watch. If the artifice like watch cannot be accounted for, without an intelligent watchmaker, how could the contrivances in nature which far surpass the human artefact in respect of complexity, mutual adaptability, and subtlety and far excel the finest products of human ingenuity, be caused by chance. He states qualificatory conditions to forestall possible objections against the argument. The argument will not be least weakened if one had never seen how a watch is made or nor if the watch sometimes goes out of order. It is patently absurd to suppose that the internal design of the watch is not there in the watch and that it is only an ascription of human mind. The argument shall not be less cogent if one did not know the mechanism of the watch. It is absurd to construe that the order is inherent in the parts of the watch, resulting from its metallic nature, such that the parts come together of their own accord to produce the watch which measures the passage of time with mathematical precision.

R.G. Swinburne seeks to provide a strongly articulated defense of design argument against objections of the critics, especially Hume. He underlines two kinds of regularity, 'regularity of co-presence', i.e. uniformities in respect of things in their spatial relationship and 'regularity of succession', i.e. uniformities in respect of things which explain their changes in time. Hume's objection rests on the observation that though the world contains striking regularities of co-presence, there are also examples of irregularities. For example, imbalance in earth's interior, species with weird physiognomy go to prove the absence of mutual adaptability of parts. Such are the instances that stultify the thesis of 'regularity of co-presence'. Such instances of 'regularity of co-presence' caused by non-human agents, are otherwise explained by natural laws (causal uniformities). But, instances of 'regularity of succession', other than those produced by the human agency, are free from any difficulty whatsoever. They refer to precise and predicate ways in which things and events behave in temporal succession. Unlike 'regularities of co-presence', 'regularities of succession', are all pervasive. Moreover, 'regularities of succession' cannot be otherwise explained scientifically. Rather, the regularity of particular succession is explained by the help of 'regularity of succession' of greater generality. They are axiomatic to science. All explanations and predictions which lend objectively to scientific enterprise assume the fact of 'regularity of succession'. So, the 'why' and 'how' of such regularities can be explained only when one postulates an agency beyond the domain wherein they (such regularities) take place. Hume argues that as a tree bestows order to other trees which spring from it and an animal bestows order to its offspring's, why cannot it be supposed that the regularities of the world are imparted to them by the antecedent conditions in the state of nature. Such arguments may hold good of the 'regularity of co-presence'. But, hardly do they apply to the 'regularity of succession' which explains not only the behaviour of the effect in relation to its cause but the totality of nature which is subject to the fixed laws. The thesis of 'cosmic designer' draws its strength from the way it explains the empirical phenomena more coherently and adequately.

According to Hume the analogy of human artefact cannot be extended to the entire universe. There is no reason why an analogy, true of the parts of nature, shall hold good of nature as a whole even if the analogy is extended to the whole, it will, at most, prove the existence of an entity who is finite and imperfect. There is no reason why one should suppose that there is only one God, instead of many Gods who have created the manifold particulars. It is also possible that 'orderliness' found in the state of universe (which constitute the butt of the teleological argument) is only temporary. Therefore, the uniformities cannot be said to disclose the essential nature of reality.

Kant extols design argument as the clearest and oldest, enjoying the support of common-sense. The perceived order, purposiveness, beauty, tempts one to think of a primordial cause without which the universe would have been a mere medley of events. But one cannot rationally proceed by analogy, from production of a given particular, to postulate a God who is the cause of the whole world of particulars. In case of a particular, both the effect and cause are available to us. Reason does not permit us to apply the category of 'causality' beyond the domain of the phenomenal. One can legitimately proceed from the state of nature to a primordial cause which is similar to human agency, responsible for finite creation. But, this hardly amounts to the proof of the existence of God. Thus, there is need of independent argument to prove the existence of God.

There have been significant attempts by the scientists to account for the origin of the universe and evolution of life. Needless to say that the scientific theories about the origin of the universe are of the nature of inferences about the primeval state on the basis of available evidence and known laws in the present. The more coherent a theory, more credible and acceptable it is. There are a group of scientists who dispute the thesis of origin of the universe, in time. They advocate 'Steady state theory' according to which the universe was in existence from eternity. Therefore, the question of explaining its origin is beside the point. They would take 'design' as facts in the state of nature, given which all explanations and predictions become possible. This thesis however stops short of explaining the design. As a result, the 'design' remains as unexplainable datum.

On the other hand, the 'Big-bang theory' traces the origin of the universe in time. The universe began with explosion or 'big-bang', as it were from a singular point and it continues to expand since then. Here, it is pertinent to ask; what is it that caused the 'big-bang'? What is the nature of the state preceding the Big-bang'? did the universe spring from the prior state of vacuum? In that case one has to accept the thesis of creation denovo i.e. something coming out of nothing, which is unacceptable to a rational mind. Did the universe create itself? Can it be explained by means of the primeval elements which are of the nature of self-unfolding particulars? It is repugnant to rational mind which insists that for every event, there must be factors necessitating its occurrence. The thesis of a self-creating universe is conceived after the analogy of a boy who, per chance, falls into a pit and escapes from it by pulling himself up by his own boot straps. If the universe could create itself energy, then the pertinent question is; What is it that caused the transition from the point of primeval unity (equilibrium), to state of multiplicity and disequilibrium ?it would be too much to suppose that matter and energy existed before the 'Big-bang' and for no reason, galvanized themselves into continual expansion. Given the vastness, complexity, orderliness of the universe, it is not conceivable that it could come out of the point of absolute utility and simplicity without the intervention of some extraneous agent. The settled law of causality is that the effect cannot be richer in content than the cause. Besides, 'causality' only provides explanation of an event retrospectively. It can hardly explain why things and beings exhibit the tendency to move to an end (*telos*).

Advocates of anthropoid principle draw our attention to certain significant coincidences at the beginning of creation for which the universe is as it is. If the initial conditions at the time of 'big-bang' were different from what they were, evolution of life would not be possible. Obviously, we would not have been here to speculate how it all came about and why it is the way it is. For example, if the gravity were stronger than what it was, then stars would have exhausted their hydrogen component much faster. As a result, protein molecules, the basic building blocks of living organisms, could not appear. Life would not have been possible. Even a causal reflection on the nature of the organic components convinces one that matter cannot organize itself to account for the evolution of RNA and DNA. Here, the hypothesis of an ordering intelligence, immanent or transcendent, constitutes the only plausible explanation.

The proponents of 'Grand Unification theory' (GUT) acknowledge the inherent inability of mind to know for certain, how the universe emerged from the state of primeval simplicity. They wonder if the universe, with its characteristic orderliness and symmetry, could unfold itself simply by chance. Such a miraculous feat of unimaginable magnitude should legitimately be attributed to creative intelligence of infinite magnitude. Any attempt to ponder over the ultimate mystery is bound to leave one, awestruck. Crown terms it as the natural miracle of our existence. To add to this, even the advocates of the theory of 'super Strong's (which presupposes creative intelligence) explain everything, microcosmic to macro-cosmic, atomic to galactic bodies, in holding that it is not infinitesimal points but infinitesimal strings that constitute the building blocks of the universe. All matter, energy and their configurations leading to the formation of compounds and all workings of nature are said to be the phenomenal expression of twitching, vibrations and interactions of these infinitesimal strings.

Here, the pointed submission of the critics need to be addressed. It is argued that any universe like that of ours, inhabited by life forms, would presuppose the fact of orderliness and symmetry because had they been absent, life would not sprout. This argument appears to be more tenable because there are many planets where there is no trace of life at all. From out of the infinite configurations like those that are found in our planet (earth) are conducive to the emergence of life. The discovered design owes its explanation to chance configurations rather than to any extraneous agency, far less an infinitely intelligent being who maneuvered the configuration in a particular manner so that life could evolve. So, all explanations in the state of nature are causal and retrospective. There is no room for explanations that are prospective or purposive (teleological). The observed design simply discloses what we are predisposed to discover. It may here be pointed that order is not only true of the actual or possible universes inhabited by life but is true of any universe whatsoever. The behaviour of all ingredients of reality, be it in atom, electron, proton, neutron, DNA or RNA disclose-intra-particular as well as inter-particular-symmetry and equilibrium which demand explanation beyond themselves. Here, the chance-hypothesis fairs poorer than the supposition that they are the result of ordering intelligence. The attempt to explain everything through causal dynamics presumes that 'causality', which is valid in the domain phenomenology, is also true of everything actual or possible. A scientifically tempered mind, misconstrues its inherent limitations to be its strength. To think that anything which is not intelligible causally is not acceptable, is to ignore the limitations of the cognitive apparatus i.e. mind. It stems from the ignorance of the truth that mind has its origin in the intermediate state of creation. Hypothetically, if the creation had a beginning, then mind came to an end, and then mind would cease to be there, long before the final dissolution. Mind can only comprehend reality of intermediary dimension. Reality in its micro-cosmic dimension (when it exists as the smaller than the smallest) and the macro-cosmic dimension (when it takes the form of the bigger than the biggest) remains, incomprehensible on account of the native limitation of mind. [11]

2.4. RELIGIOUS EXPERIENCE

The description of religion and its experience is a scientific undertaking for it is necessary to look at facts dispassionately and objectively. We must penetrate beyond what is publicly observable. Though there may be difficulties in our appreciating fully the content and quality of mystical and other forms of religious experience, there is a sense in which we can deal with them objectively. A religious experience involves some kind of perception of the invisible world, or involves a perception that some visible person or thing is a manifestation of the invisible world.[12]

Existence of God is most often sought to be proved not by appealing to reason but to 'religious experience'. A truth-claim stands in need of justification and more so, the truth-claims in religion. In other words, the proponent of truth-claim bears the onus of stating the grounds or rationale behind the claim. The controversy with regard to the existence of God veers around the truth-claim that 'God exists'. In the absence of objective, corroborative experience or justification, critics find constrained to accord it the status of a knowledge-claim. In response to this, theologians appeal to the experience of the religious people, mystics and realized souls who testify to the knowledge-claim that 'God exists'. In this sense, reality of God is claimed to be at par with the reality of other objects with the sole difference that the former, being non-spatio temporal, differs in its intrinsic nature from those that exist in space and time. Since, God is radically different from the 'particulars' in space and time, the modes of experiencing Him, also, differ characteristically. Religious experience is said to be of the nature of 'I-Thou' encounter where the object 'Thou' is none other than God, the Infinite, the Transcendent. Empirical experience is of the nature 'I-It' encounter where the object 'It' is a finite. So, both in 'I-Thou' and "I-It' encounter, subject remaining the same, the objects of experience are intrinsically different. That explains why the nature of religious experience turns out to be characteristically distinct from empirical experience.

Religious experience is claimed to be mystical, ineffable and transient. Any attempt to describe that which is beyond categorization, is bound to be futile. In empirical experience, the subject and object remain distinct. In religious experience, the 'knower' and the 'known' lose their respective identity or separateness. There is the feeling of ecstasy only, without there being the consciousness of 'subjects' experiencing the object'. Though it comes at the end of long psychophysical preparedness, one doesn't know, when shall it come? Whom does it come? There is an element of abruptness with which the individual is pushed to a state where the finite consciousness opens itself up to the transcendent. The experience is so overwhelmingly authentic that it needs no extraneous evidence to get it corroborated. Concepts and categories employed to describe the transactions in day-to-day experience fail to provide faithful account of it squarely because of the very nature of experience and the inherent limitations of concepts. Such experience remains significant only for the experiment. This doesn't, of course mean that such experiences are out subjective. No religious man claims that such experiences are prerogative of a few. Rather, they are essentially meant for all those who are fraught with limitations. It holds out the hope that anyone and everyone can achieve it by personal endeavour. It can be achieved by any mortal. But when it would occur, depends upon where one stands in course of the journey across lives. For someone, even whole life of penance may not be adequate and for some other, mere word, look and touch of the master or even a small happening may be enough to transport one to the state of spiritual ecstasy.

Mystics, prophets, saints and seers unanimously certify about the reality of the transcendent. They relate about their experience of the numinous, noumenal which every man should cherish to have by following the religious way. Nature and structure of religious experience is vastly different from the everyday experience of ours. That's explains why, one is filled with awe, wonder and ecstasy which are too very profound for expression through ordinary language. What bothers a rational mind is the diversity of religious experience. Such trans-empirical experiences are common to monotheistic, polytheistic and non-theistic religions. But religions differ widely with regard to the nature of such experience. This makes room for diversity of religious faiths and followings. If truth is one and human beings possess similar cognitive apparatus why is it that the same reality is described in so very different ways. There is difference between having an experience and description of it. It is possible that though they experience the singular truth, descriptions of them differ widely. Truth is one but expressed in diverse ways (*ekamsad viprāh vahudā vadanti*). Every description involves interpretation. It is but natural that when the same experience is sought to be expressed through language, they differ widely. But such inevitable differences, do not, in the least, undermine the authenticity of such experience.

Religious statements are not merely description of what is taking place but contain justification of a transcendental reality or a transcendental order. According to critics, such truth-claims eventually, turn out to be belief-claims in so far as they fall short of the criterion of 'objectivity' and 'universality'. If religious experience is, in principle, ineffable, nothing can be said about its truth or falsity. Unless one lets others know what such experience is about, it is not possible to go about in settling its truth-claim. In citing religious experience as authentic, there is the dual claim that such experience is genuine and it points to the existence of God which makes such experience possible. Critics would submit that there is no logical passage from the fact of experience to the claim that it is a faithful presentation of what it is the experience of. In case of an illusory experience, for example the experience of silver in shell, there is no difficulty if one says that one had the experience of silver. But the truth-claim that it is a piece of silver makes room for difficulties. It is possible that there is no real 'silver' even though one has the experience of 'silver'. To say that there is a silver which causes the experience of silver, one has to go beyond the experience in order to be sure that it is really silver which caused the experience of silver. It is discovered that what was there all along, is not silver but a shell, causing the erroneous experience of the silver, the truth-claim that 'it is silver' stands stultified. In other words, occurrence of experience, as such, doesn't establish the objective correlation between a 'reality' which causes the experience and the 'experience'. One has to have a criterion by which one should be in a position to distinguish between a genuine experience from illusory or hallucinatory experience. Even if it is conceded that in religious experience, one opens oneself to the 'Thou', establishes oneself in the numinous and such experience is authentic, there must be some way to let others know that it is not an instance of self-description or hallucination. How to counter the observation of the critics that religious experiences have psychological or naturalistic explanation? For which they can hardly be taken as descriptive account of the encounter with the divine. Claims of religious men and, mystics have to be given credence only on the score that such experiences have logic of their own. Therefore, they cannot be classed along with the experience of the phenomenal. They are self-authentic on account of the elements of certitude, clarity and self-evidence. While pointing to the certitude of the 'mystical' they indicate the limit of the non-mystical or empirical. Nonetheless, in order to certify a piece of cognition as objective, one has to verify it by oneself i.e. undergo the cognition by oneself. Besides, such cognition must lend itself to be verified by anyone and everyone. The theologians submit that religious experience is objective as it contains tacit invitation to one and all to experience it by them. One cannot have an experience on behalf of another. For example, one cannot see by the eyes of the other or understand by the mind of another. The objectivity of religious experience and the truth-claims thereof, follow from the clarity, authenticity and certitude of such experience which can be vouchsafed by anyone and everyone who has the competence to undergo such experience.[13]

Existence of God is, often, sought to be proved by appeal to workability of the 'belief in God', in practice. It is observed that belief in a God who is the creator, preserver and destroyer, omniscient, omnipotent and omnipresent entity, the moral governor of the universe (dispenser of reward and punishment) makes significant difference to the individual and social life of man. God-consciousness serves as the moral censor who constrains one from following the path of immorality and evil. 'Belief in God' serves as a unfailing prop for people in moments diffidence, despair and agony. Critics dispute such contention by drawing our attention to contrary evidence. They show how belief in God has been largely responsible for perpetrating persecution, internecine feuds and communal discord, at large. It may here be noted that such instances only go to show the dysfunction of religion. The illicit fallout of religions is the result of lack of genuine belief in god, our half-hearted convictions. It simply points to human fallibility in cultivating faith in God.

There seems to be no logical passage from workability of a belief to the claim as to its truth. Sometimes, make-beliefs and even false-beliefs prove to be more expedient and salutary than 'truth'. If a 'belief' turns out to be useful it simply means that it is worth having. But the claim that it is true has to be substantiated independently by appeal to facts. Thus, utility or disutility of a belief is independent of its truth and falsity. If faith in God proves useful in life, it does not conclusively prove that god exists. In scientific parlance, a hypothesis is verified more or less by seeing how it is compatible with experience and workability in practice. 'Hypothesis' is a provisional supposition which attains the status of truth or law, after being verified. God is therefore not a willful concoction of clever minds but a spontaneous postulation of the unsullied minds, signifying deeper necessity of our being, implicitly pointing to the reality of such state, by attaining which the irresistible quest for harmony and bliss comes to an end.

Though God is acknowledged as a singular entity there are multiplicities of belief in God. If belief in God entails his existence should we not rationally accept the existence of different Gods corresponding to different beliefs? It is held that even though God is one, it is conceived differently depending on the psychological makeup of the people. Religious texts in India reveal how God comes to be related to the individual as the offspring (*Yoshada in vatsalyabhava*), servitor (*Hanuman in dasyabhava*), consort (*Radha in madhurabhava*) and so on. Though God is one and eternal, he is viewed in different ways. It is a fact that belief in God induces the non-believer to lead a good life. A belief doesn't become true simply because it works. It is more reasonable to say that it works because it is true. A belief becomes true when it is in conformity with reality, irrespective of its utility value. Even granting the religious beliefs have salutary effect on human conduct, nothing would follow about the veracity of religious claims. Can one not think of cultivating a good moral life without belief in God? Is religion necessary for good conduct? In fact, there have been significant efforts to show that morality is independent of religion. The soundness of the claim can partly be ascertained by empirical survey across the globe, in order to see whether and to what extent, adherence to religious faith do invariably lead to socially useful behaviour and whether all moral acts are motivated by religious faith.

Pascal works out a rational defence in favour of the existence of God purely on pragmatic grounds. He argues that if God really exists and we do not believe that 'He exist', we stand to lose a great deal but hardly gain much. If God does not exist and we believe that 'He exists' we gain much but lose a little. So it is better to believe that 'He is because while weighing gain and loss, it is the believer who stands to gain and loses a little.

But this does not reflect the true spirit behind existence-claims about God. If God exists, it is so, prior to our act of believing Him. Existence of God is prior, and our belief or disbelief is posterior phenomena. 'Belief in God' refers to the initial stage of the journey. It matures into knowledge of God when one realizes God or attains Godhood. Religious experience is open to verification like any other experience. It is but natural that unlike other particulars in our everyday experience, God-experience calls for appropriate competence on the part of the individual. Attitude of faith, surrender, moral competence and sincere longing, are called for in respect of God experience, as much as sensory-competence is necessary for experience of the phenomenal, the spatio-temporal.[14]

Miracle is an event which defies explanation in terms of the laws of nature. It confounds human mind as one fails to account for it in the way other facts or events are sought to be explained. In the absence of naturalistic explanation, miracle is dubbed as a super-natural event; it must have a cause which is super-natural. There is no oddity involved in postulating a super-natural cause for a super-natural event. Thus, God is invoked to account for such super-natural phenomena called 'miracle'. Life of mystics, saints or realised souls abound in accounts of miracles. 'Being present at two different places simultaneously', 'healing the (terminally) sick by mere touch or words', 'raising the dead from the grave', 'giving graphic account of remote past and seeing into the distant future', are instances of miracles. They are construed as the living testimony of divinity enactment. God-hood is ascribed to one through whom the miracles are wrought. Miracle is, therefore, conceived as God's intervention in course of things. If he wishes a lame can cross mountains, a dumb becomes eloquent.

Occurrence of miracles, through attested by a few, is accepted wholeheartedly by the believing community. Again, there are others who are disposed not to believe anything which is not certified by experience (sense-experience) or attested by reason. They question the vercity of such miraculous happenings and even, go to the extent of maintaining that the concept of 'miracle' is not rationally tenable. On the one hand, there are those who believe in miracles simply on the testimony of those who, in their opinion, could not have gone wrong because of their accredited status otherwise. On the other hand, there are those who are not prepared to accept such truth claims howsoever clear, coherent and corroborative the testimony might appear to be.

Critics, first of all, question whether the notion of 'miracle' can be assigned any meaning at all. Any meaningful event is explainable at least, in principle, in term of causal uniformities. It is not reasonable to view a happening as miraculous simply because one does not know of nature. Knowledge does not have a fixed boundary. The frontier of knowledge is ever expanding. Many things which were accepted as articles of faith, have found explanation with later discoveries. For example, more rational explanation are coming forth to account for the so called miracles like, 'bringing things into existence out of nothing' and 'making things disappear', extra sensory phenomena like telepathy clairvoyance etc. A putative event must not be taken as miracle simply because it is not explainable by laws of nature. If an event is not explainable by the known laws of nature, from this it does not follow that it cannot, in principle, be explained by any law whatsoever which may be discovered in future. Under this interpretation, no event as such, can be taken as a miracle because we cannot, *a priority* draws a limit to what can be known. If miracle is construed as an event which does not have actual or possible explanation in terms of the laws of nature, the very concept of 'super-natural' shall be a misnomer. One would not know what a miracle would be like if it does not have an explanation in terms of causal uniformities.

Miracle enjoy acceptance among the laity and the credulous simply because people, by and large, have the tendency to remain awe struck and lend credence to the marvels that baffle human mind. To say this, is simply to offer psychological explanation for the genesis of belief in miracles. Hume points out that given the truth-claims about miracles, the rational temper of the mind, demand disbelief rather than belief. He says down a stringent criterion before accepting that a miracle is veridical. Truth-claim about miracle is genuine if and only if its falsehood or negation cannot be proved. No testimony is sufficient to establish the veracity of a miracle-claim unless its falsehood is proved to be a more miraculous than it. Even if miracle is attested by some and there are reasons for not believing it to be so. It is submitted in nature and there can be no objective evidence in support of the contention that they really did occur. In other words, all testimony whatsoever, fall short of conclusive proof. The rare and sporadic freaks called 'miracle' cannot compel rational minds to accept their truth, unless otherwise, it is uniformly experienced and certified against objective conditions by bias-free minds. Community of believers are found to subscribe to the belief in miracles unanimously. On account of weakness of human mind for the super-natural, it is taken for a ride by propagators of miracles who otherwise command unconditional trust and veneration of the people, the legacy, once in place, continues to be imbibed by succeeding generations. It is also argued that if occurrence of miracle means the intervention of God in course of nature, why does not God, the omnipotent and benevolent being, prevent the catastrophes which take away good and the bad, devilish and the saintly in one sweep. Why heal one or some? Why not all?

Why not prevent suffering? so that there is no further need for redemption from suffering. The proponents of 'miracle' carry the onus of showing that miraculous happenings are objective and that they are not explainable by any natural law whatsoever. Critics feel constrained to accept miracle as an event because any event, *per se*, owes its explanation to the causal antecedents which, in turn, are meaningful against the backdrop of uniformities of nature. A person who is established in infinitude acquires occult powers to become smaller than the smallest, bigger than the biggest, summon things into existence by mere wish and so on. But attaining such power is never claimed as the privilege of a few. It holds out the hope for everyone. Such things appear as normal for one who lives on that height. It means that miracles have dynamics of their own, intrinsically different from the causal dynamics that explain events in the state of nature. To try to understand miracles by the logic of the phenomenal is to commit category mistake. In the language of Wittgenstein, one cannot be played by the rules of another. It has been aptly said that *the logic of the Infinite is magic for the finite.*

CHAPTER - 3

RELIGIOUS KNOWLEDGE AND LANGUAGE

Modern endeavour in the philosophy of religion has been engaged with problems established by the distinctively religious applications of language. Two main issues are taken up during the discussions. The former, that which was well-known amongst the medieval thinkers and with the help of new techniques it is still being diligently investigated. It deals with the various nuances that arise when trying to describe God. The latter, also has a long history and over the years has been sharpened with the help of analytical philosophy. Its concerns are the basic functions of religious language, in particular to some religious statements that seem to be factual assertions. 'God loves mankind' refers to a "special" kind of fact, religious in nature and not scientific or could it be a different function altogether? Each of these differences will be taken up in the order mentioned above.

Terms applied to God in religious discourses are most often being used in a special way that differs from the ordinary contexts of those words. Here are a few examples:

1) 'Great is the God' is not here meant that God is vast or enormous; in this context God is exceptionally outstanding and has a noble character.
2) 'The Lord spoke unto Joshua' does not mean that a physical person named Lord spoke to Joshua.
3) 'God is good' does not mean that he can be bad at time like us human beings, his nature transcends dualities and thus he cannot be judged.

These examples go to show that there has been a long shift of meaning between the normal secular use of these words and their theological usage.

Between the theological and secular usage of a word, the secular meaning is primary because it was developed first. This completely changes when we use the same secular word to God. For example the "word love" whether ("Eros" or "Agape") expresses a range of actions from holding hands, love-making, parental love, etc. This kind of love is embodied but what then is disembodied love? Can we ever know its existence? Similar questions arise in relation to the other divine attributes.

3.1. RELIGIOUS LANGUAGE

Religious discourse is characteristically different from empirical discourse. They differ with regard to the nature of truth-claims. Descriptive language makes truth-claims about the empirical, the phenomenal, and the spatio-temporal. Truth-value of a descriptive statement is determined by appeal to what is the case i.e. how the world is like. In other words, whether a proposition is true or false depends upon the nature of reality. Religious claims are also truth-claims with the sole difference that they purport to describe a reality which is otherwise not available to sense-experience or intelligible in terms of the logic of the descriptive discourse. Every truth claim is a claim to 'objectivity'. Truth claim is objective if it is either true or false, independent of the subject who makes the truth-claim. A proposition is neither true nor false, as such. It becomes either true or false by virtue of the relationship that obtains between the propositional claim and the state of affair. Even though the religious discourse differs from empirical discourse in respect of the nature of reality it purports to describe, it mostly makes use of the language i.e. the subjects, predicates, verbs, attributes and qualifiers, of the latter. Propositional claims in theological discourse are not contested by the non-cognitivists. According to them religious claims being meaningless (non-cognitive) the question of their truth or falsity is beside the point. Before determining whether a proposition is true or false, one must know what the purported claim is about, one also doesn't know how to go about in settling the truth-value of such seeming truth-claim. Though religious claims have the semblance of conveying something deep and profound, they do not convey anything at all. Though grammatically sound, they are semantically odd. Experience is central to the intelligibility of a discourse. So, they contend that all meaningful propositions must be ultimately analysable into sense-experience.

3.1.1. Principle of Verifiability

The sources of knowledge contain justification of knowledge-claims. The way 'knowledge' arises is also the way by which a knowledge-claim (arising thereof) is sought to be justified. Human thesis of meaningfulness was taken up by the positivists in form of the 'verifiability principle of meaning'. According to positivists, a meaningful proposition must be either synthetic i.e. about matters of fact or analytic i.e. about relationship among concepts. For example, 'bachelors are happy' provides information about bachelors. It becomes either true or false, depending upon what is the case. But the proposition 'bachelors are unmarried males' remains true, independent of what the reality is like. By mere analysis of the meaning of the terms in the proposition, one can know that it is true and necessarily, so. They are devoid of factual content i.e. empirically uninformative. On the other hand, a synthetic proposition is about matters of fact. So, its truth value i.e. truth and falsity, is dependent upon what the world is like. Judged by this criterion, propositions in theology do not fall into either of the categories. They are neither analytic nor synthetic. Propositions in theology are claimed to provide significant information about an aspect of reality which is not otherwise available to sense-experience. So, they are not analytic by the very admission of the theologian. Positivists contend that they are not synthetic either because they do not satisfy the 'criterion of verifiability'. Truth-claim in theology is neither verified as a matter fact nor is it verifiable in principle. One cannot think of actual or possible situation which would render them conclusively true or false or even, contingently true or false. On the contrary, the theologian would claim that they are not true but necessarily true. According to positivists, only analytic propositions are necessarily true and such necessity is secured on account of their factual emptiness. A theologian seeks to retain analyticity (necessity and universality) and syntheticity (factuality) of a proposition at the same time.

3.1.2. Principle of Falsifiability

A theologian contends that propositions in religious discourse are verifiable by 'experience' though of a different kind. The falsifiability theory of meaning states that a proposition worth the name must be falsifiable, if and only if, it is possible to think of an actual or possible situation which would render it conclusively false. This is based on the basic presupposition that every proposition must have a specific or determinate sense. 'Specificity' is essential to the concept of meaning. That, which seeks to convey everything about everything, conveys nothing. In other words, a proposition which is compatible with all possible state of affairs is devoid of sense.

"Once two explorers where traveling and they stumbled upon a clearing in the jungle. It was filled with weeds and beautiful flowers. The first explorer is of the opinion that a gardener tends the flowers, while the other disagrees and says there is no gardener. To justify their respective contentions they pitched a tent and kept a vigilant watch. No gardener could be seen so the first explorer says that the gardener must be invisible. To see if this is the case they brought dogs and set up an electrified barbed wire around the clearing. They waited a while but nothing happened, the first explorer says 'He must be invisible, insensible to an electric shock who comes stealthily to take care of the garden'. Reacting to this the other explorer says that there remains nothing of the original assertion that there is a gardener. How does the invisible and non-sensible gardener differ from no gardener at all, as asserted by the second explorer?"

Proposition in theology are claimed to be true, irrespective of what the world is like. One cannot think of an actual or possible situation which would render it false conclusively. They are claimed to be not only true but necessarily true and universally, so.

3.1.3. Principle of Translatability

In view of the inadequacies of the 'verifiability' and 'falsifiability' as criteria of meaning. Hempel advances 'translatability' as a criterion of meaning. According to this criterion a proposition is meaning if and only if it is translatable to empricistic language. An empiricist language is one which is constituted by observation-predicates, logical connectives and observation-sentences. An observation predicate is one which describes an observation characteristics. An observation-characteristic signifies the presence and absence of a characteristic, known by sense experience. Since theological proposition are not translatable to the observations-sentences, they are considered as patently nonsensical. Verifiability, falsifiability and translatability have one thing in common i.e. appeal to 'experience' where 'experience' is taken to mean 'sense-experience'.[2]

3.1.4. Theological Statement as Conative

According to Braithwaite, theological expressions, though non-cognitive, are profoundly significant. A meaningful expression need not necessarily be cognitive. He underlines the non-cognitive functions of language. Religious discourse is predominantly intentional. Theological proposition expresses one's intention to embrace a way of life. Unlike indicative propositions, they do not describe states of affair. They are expressive of one's commitment to follow a value-centric life. Thus, they are not cognitive but conative, in so far as they express the mindset and implicit commitment of the individual to live a life, wedded to values. Though at the surface, they appear to convey information about the supernatural, they are forms of self-disclosure. The statement that 'we, all are the offspring's of God, discloses the attitude and intention of the speaker to treat everything and everyone. In this respect, religious discourse has affinity with moral discourse. Similarly, the expression 'god is love' means that one is inclined to see every incident, however painful or dreadful, as the expression of god's benevolent design. Similarly, the normative expression that 'truth telling is virtue' means that one is predisposed to be truthful and eschew lies, even though the circumstances tend to constrain one to take to falsehood. Braithwaite underlines that all the religions of the world have the common goal of persuading the believers to live a life, impregnated with values. Stories, mythologies, beliefs and practices are bound to be different because a particular religion seeks to address his contemporaries with their characteristic problems. Religious, therefore, have differences only at the surface but not at the core. The stories and parables are nothing but conceptual artifice which, on the one hand, deter one from unrighteous life and motivate one to lead the life of righteousness, on the other. Ne religion differs from another not in terms of fundamental visions or basic truth-claims but in terms of stories, parables and mythologies. They are of the nature of improvisations that seek to infuse the sense of values and the urgency of pursuing them.

Needless to say that a God-centric society is more stable and harmonious than the one where people by and large, subscribe to matter-centric values. It is possible that a society where 'matter' is taken as the ultimate reality and the only reality is economically prosperous. But in such a society, people behave like intelligent savages wherein every action of the individual is promoted by the desire for sensuous pleasure or selfish interest. Worthwhileness of the stories does not lie in their historicity but in their function to motivate the lesser mortals to lead a value-centric life. A believer is always reminded that though 'matter' is real, it is not the only reality. Though material concerns are to be attended to, one has also to remain alive to the demands of the mind and soul. Thus, the significance of religious discourse lies in its workability by way of helping people to live a life of love, mutual trust and sacrifice. Society that revolves around the vision of fatherhood of God and brotherhood of man, shall lead to a state where shall be lesser discord and greater understanding, lesser animosity and greater love, lesser mistrust and greater trust. But a devout believer doesn't go along with Braithwaite's explanation of religious language. In the religious framework, god is the very ground of all existence, actual and possible. If God is seen as a mere conceptual construction, belief in God would be nothing but an instance of make-belief. It is argued that beliefs do not become true because they are workable but that beliefs are workable because they are true. A life can never be lived with success and satisfaction simply on the strength of a make-belief, howsoever profound it may be.

3.1.5. Theological Statements as Symbolic

Randall underlines the distinctive functions of religious symbols. Expressions in religious discourse are non-representative. They are meaningful not in terms of what they describe or represent but in terms of their characteristics functions. Society is not a mere togetherness of individuals. There are certain common bonds which bind people together whereby they participate in the act of caring, sharing and sacrificing for one another. Individuals differ from one another in respect of their attitudes, aptitudes, vocations and priorities. A stable social order is one wherein people, irrespective of their differences, share a common ethos and live towards common goal. Religious language evoke positive emotions, sentiments and feelings in the individual which goad them to socially useful actions. Besides, they reinforce the sense of commitment to pursue a common goal. What is important is that individuals should integrate their cognitive, conative affective faculties and participate in a shared living in order to achieve the common goal. Randall brings into focus the non-cognitive as well as the secular aspects of religion. Ordinary symbols are communicative whereas religious symbols are evocative. Factual statement is concerned with the spatio-temporal whereas a truth-claim in religion draw our attention to an alternative dimension of reality which is termed as order of the 'splendour'. According to Randall religious symbols stimulate different kind of awareness and open up a new world which is not otherwise accessible to 'sense' and 'reason'. Religious moot certain ideas which serve as inexhaustible source of inspiration. They impart meaning to human strivings which otherwise appear to be mechanical and monotonous. Truth-claims in religions prove to be socially expedient as they help people resolve differences and contradictions. 'God' is the most sacred concept in religion which lends meaning to other ancillary concepts such as, soul, rebirth and immorality. Symbols employed in religious discourse give meaning to religion as a form of life and remain valid in terms of their socially useful functions. The pragmatic interpretation of religious language undermines the ontological significance of God, soul and liberation, vouchsafed by the theologians. The fact that the religions prove to be practically expedient do not undermine the ontological significance of religious truths and experiences. Randall travels half-way, as he dwells on the function of religious language only, without addressing the ontology of truth-claims in the religious discourse.[3]

3.1.6. Language Game Theory

A third non-cognitive influential outlook of religious language is taken from the later philosophy of Ludwig Wittgenstein (1889-1995) and has been further developed by D.Z. Phillips and others. Language of religion and science according to this view constitute different 'language games'. These games are the linguistic aspects of different 'forms of life'. For example the 'form of life' for Hinduism would be the Hindu language and for Christians it would be the Christian language, and each of these have their own criteria which helps determining what is true and false within their respective discourses. The various 'language games' and their 'forms of life' make a given 'language game' invulnerable to critic from outside that particular game or discourse of language and life. Thus religious utterances are unaffected by scientific and other nonreligious comments.

Traditional Christian discourse talks about the first man and woman, Adam and Eve, and their fall from paradise that made them along with their descendants guilty before God. The Neo-Wittgenstein theory of religious language says that such a way of talking does not clash with the scientific theory that humans are descended from a single primal pair.

To compare religion with observational facts and scientific research and to require its convictions to be compatible with those facts would make it irreligious. The 'form of life' of religion is autonomous; it has its own 'language game' making it invulnerable to critic from outside that particular game or discourse of language and life. Thus religious utterances are unaffected by scientific and other nonreligious comments. The notion that religion has the power to reveal to us the actual structure of reality, a larger scheme of existence than our present reality, is on this view a basic mistake. One has to add, however, that if this is a mistake it is one that all the great religious teachers and founders have made!

D,Z. Phillips has applied the view of religion as a distinctive language-game to two themes in particular: prayer and immortality. I shall use the latter to illustrate further this proposal in the philosophy of religion. Whereas the Christian belief in "the life everlasting" has normally been understood as a belief about our destiny after bodily death, and thus as a belief that is factually either true or false and that will, if true, be confirmed in future human experience, Phillips sees it as having no such implications. The soul is the moral personality.

The term 'He'd sell his soul for money' is a moral observation about the speaker; it expresses the fallen state of that person. This remark doesn't involve any philosophical theory about a duality in human nature.[4]

God being a disembodied entity the question arises how can we know his divine nature? Saint Thomas Aquinas declares we don't know. With the help of analogy he tried to indicate the relation between the words and their meaning when applied both to man and God (on the basis of revelation). Analogy lacks the proficiency to explore and map the infinite divine nature; it can only provide a framework for certain limited statements about God.

The Catholic theologian, Friedrich von Hugel (1852-1925) an Austrian layman speaks of the faint, dim, and confused awareness that a dog has of its master. He claims that if the source and object of religion both be true it will still not be clear enough for him to understand it. He compares his finite reality to his dog's finite reality and wonders how much of his reality does his dog actually understand. He says 'the obscurity of my life to my dog must thus be greatly exceeded by the obscurity of the life of God to me'. Similarly he says if religion be right we must admit the superior nature of God. He says 'of God of His reality and life, so different and superior, so unspeakably more rich and alive, than is, or ever can be, my own life and reality.[5]

Wittgenstein would agree with the positivists that religious language is non-cognitive, as propositions therein do not describe the matters of fact. But on this account, a religious statement cannot be dubbed as meaningless. 'Description' is a basic function but not the sole function of language. Language is used not only to describe the world or relationship among ideas but also for doing various other functions such as; telling stories, cutting jokes, speculating, playing, acting, thinking, blessing, cursing, greeting, praying etc. The words are like tools in a toolbox which can be used for very many purposes.

The same expression may have different shades of meaning in different contexts. Meaning is context-specific. Language is context-bound. Words as such, divested of context, are nothing but mere ink marks or sounds. They acquire meaning, when employed in a context. What an expression means depends upon the way it is used. For example, the word 'truth' in the religious context connotes the ultimate reality e.g. God is truth. In common parlance, 'truth' means a 'fact' e.g. 'police is trying to unearth the truth'. 'Truth', for a logician, means one of the 'truth-values' of a proposition. So, what 'truth' means would depend upon the context of its use.

To bring out the significance of the context Wittgenstein invokes the analogy of 'language game' just as a game is played with its characteristic set of rules, each discourse has its own logic. In order to understand a particular it is necessary that one is in know of the logic of the discourse, just as, in order to play a game it is necessary that the player understands and assimilates the rules of the game. One game cannot be played by the rulers of another. One cannot play football by the rulers of cricket nor vice-versa. Similarly, one language cannot be understood by the logic of another. Language of religion has the logic of its own. So it doesn't make sense to understand religious discourse by the logic of descriptive discourse. As playing a game, calls for sense of participation on the part of the players, using a language calls for participation in a mode of life. To use a language is to embrace a mode of life.

D. Z. Phillips employs the Wittgenstein vision to bring out the logic of religious language. The meaning of religious language is to be found in religious mode living. Meaning is context-bound or discourse-bound religious statements should neither be interpreted literally nor in abstraction but in the way are they used in the complex web of life. The meaning of religious statements and the validity of truth-claims therein, are to be discussed and contested only against the religious mode of living. A hypothesis or a theory in religion is different from those in science. The religious hypothesis that the created universe owes its origin to cosmic intelligence (creator God) doesn't come in conflict with the Darwinian hypothesis that human species have evolved from the unicellular organisms through the process of natural selection. The way a religious statement is rendered meaningful and valid is not the way a scientific hypothesis is substantiated. Concepts like God, soul are not mental constructions nor are they instances of make-belief but are indicative of their semantic moorings in the religious way of life. God is not the creation of our fancy. It is not defined into existence by a believer. Religious symbols have their semantic autonomy within the religious discourse and religious mode of living. When the words are abstracted out of context and their meaning is sought to be deciphered in an alien context or discourse, one commits the categorical fallacy.

One cannot add or subtract meaning from such symbols. Having been born to a religious tradition, one imbibes certain values, beliefs which prove to be objective and existentially expedient, no less than any other objective belief. Phillips offers the hermeneutics of certain concepts of religion like God, eternity etc. The meaning of God is to be found, by looking into the way in which people, having faith in God, find themselves differently related to the so-called others. For them love, service, sacrifice become moral compulsions. Similarly, 'eternity' is not to be understood as continuity of life after death but living a life of bliss and contentment.[6]

3.1.7. Religious Language as Non-cognitive

When people declare facts, they are using language cognitively. For example 'one plus one equals two' or 'the population of India is 132.42 crores'. Such cognitive utterances can be either true or false. There are also utterances that are neither true nor false, theological sentences are of such kind. 'God loves mankind' raises two questions:

Religious people normally see this kind of theological sentence as true and cognitive. They don't necessarily pause to consider if there is a difference between scientific facts that are obtained through sense experience and religious facts aren't obtained through sense experience and thus fall short of being actual facts. Contemporary theories treat religious language as non-cognitive.

There is no doubt that as a matter of historical fact religious people have normally believed such statements as 'God loves mankind' to be not only cognitive but also true. Without necessarily pausing to consider the difference between religious facts and the facts disclosed through sense perception and the sciences, ordinary believers within the Judaic-Christian tradition have assumed that there are religious realities and facts, and that their own religious convictions are concerned with such.

A growing number of theories treat religious language as non-cognitive. Professor J.H Randall, like Tillich, indicates how religious symbols can be used in the service of naturalism. Randall conceives of religion as a human activity, like other activities, art, philosophy and science each have their own special contributions to make to man's culture. The distinctive material with which religion works is composed of symbols and myths.

According to Randall what is important to recognize is that religious symbols belong with social and artistic symbols that are both non-cognitive. Such symbols indicate a peculiar function rather than some external thing that can be indicated apart from their function. Religious symbols have a fourfold function. Their primary function is to rouse the emotions and stir men to action, their secondary function is to stimulate cooperative action and thus bind a community, their tertiary function is to communicate qualities of experience that cannot be expressed by ordinary language, their quaternary function is to clarify, foster and evoke man's experience of the world, also called, 'order of splendor' or the Divine. In describing this last function Randall says that it opens our hearts to new qualities, it teach us how to find the Divine and shows us visions of his grandeur and splendor.

Randall's position represents a radical shift from the traditional assumptions of Western religion. When he speaks of 'finding the Divine' and being shown 'visions of the Divine', Randall does not imply that the Divine exists independently of the human mind. The Divine then is nothing more than a symbol, a mental construct, a fleeting ripple of imagination in a tiny corner of the cosmos only as long as men exist. This way of thinking is widespread today in the academic study of religion, the distinction between god and religion has become blurred, God now is only a subtopic within the larger subject of religion. God is then defined in terms of religion, as one of the concepts with which it works, rather than religion being defined by God, as the field of people's outlook to a supernatural being.[7]

The switch from God to religion as the focus of a wide range of discourses has also changed the type of questions asked. The questions previously asked were whether God exists and if he is real, on the other hand it is obvious that religion exists, so the questions asked now are whether it serves human life and if it ought to be cultivated and developed. The question of the truth of religious beliefs has now fallen into the background and the issue of their practical usefulness has come into the foreground.

At a more popular level religion is widely regarded, in a psychological mode, as a human activity whose general function is to enable the individual to achieve harmony both internally and in relation to the environment. One of the distinctive ways in which religion fulfils this function is by preserving and promoting certain great ideas or symbols that possess the power to invigorate our finer aspirations. The most important and enduring of these symbols is God. Thus, at both academic and popular levels God is, in effect, defined in terms of religion, as one of the concepts with which religion works, rather than religion being defined in terms of God, as the field of people's varying responses to a real supernatural being.

The seeking for the truths of religious beliefs are no longer the subject of concern, the practical usefulness of such beliefs is what has now occupied the center of scrutiny. Is this change natural to an age of wanting faith? John Stuart Mill, an atheist, in his famous essay '*The Utility of Religion*' makes such an analysis.

The question of utility doesn't arise unless people cease to rely on it. For example people do not question their surroundings unless there is a reason to do so. Things intrinsically have an utility and we don't question its utility unless we cease to believe it has a purpose. The utility of religion also did not need to be asserted until the arguments for its truths ceased to be convincing. John Stuart Mill in the '*The Utility of Religion*' tries to put forth an argument for the utility of religion to the three kinds of believers:

1) Non-believers, to induce them to practice a well meant hypocrisy.
2) Semi-believers, to make them avert their eyes from what might possibly shake their unstable belief.
3) People in general, to abstain from expressing any doubt they may feel.

The current emphasis on utility rather than the truth shows a profound difference between taking what is useful to us from God and serving and worshipping him. God if he be real is our creator who is infinitely superior to us but we in dealing with religions and their beliefs occupy the appraiser's role and have subsumed God, our creator, within that which we appraise. While dealing with religions, within which God is an idea, a concept whose history can be traced, analyzed, defined, and even revised! God then is not omnipotent, as in biblical thought, he is impotent and thus cannot be our creator.

Over time religion according to some dominant views became essentially an aspect of human culture. This view is put in contrast with other modern and prevalent views such as naturalism, scientism, and positivism which over a short period of time have achieved a tremendous growth due to the application of the scientific methods and the rejection of God as a phenomenon available for scientific study. God is not a phenomenon science can study and thus religion takes on this task. There can be a history, a psychology, a phenomenology, sociology and a comparative study of religion. Thus God and religion become the center of intensive investigation within this complex phenomenon of religion.[8]

3.2. RELIGIOUS SYMBOLS

Language is the most convenient medium to share our ideas, experience and codify them for future reference. Language-use consists of creative manipulation of signs and symbols. Language has two distinguishable aspects, namely, 'content' and 'form'. Experience, ideas or meaning, form the 'content' whereas the signs, symbols, metaphors, analogies, similes etc. Constitute the 'form'. As is the 'content' so is the 'form'. Different levels of reality demand different forms of language for being communicated.

3.2.1. Sign and Symbol

In common parlance, there is hardly any clear distinction between 'Sign' and 'Symbol'. In science and mathematics, the notion of addition, subtractions etc. are represented through signs. Language is said to be a body of verbal sign i.e. words. The distinction between 'sign' and 'symbol' is significant. Both 'sign' and 'symbol', point beyond themselves. To understand a sign or a symbol is to read off what it stands for. As such, a sign or symbol is a visible mark or sound. It acquires meaning only when it is co-related with something, other than itself. The same expression could be both a sign and a symbol. 'Red light' on the traffic is a 'sign' which means that the road is closed. The 'red light' outside the operation theatre means that the operation is on. But the 'red flag' may be a symbol of a revolutionary creed. The relationship between sign and what is signified, is extrinsic whereas the relationship between the 'symbol' and the 'symbolized' is intrinsic. This is also true of most of the words of language wherein a particular word is used as a matter of linguistic convention to refer to something or signify a set of meanings. But when we take 'white' as a symbol of 'peace' or 'red' as the symbol of 'dynamism', we do not do it as a matter of convention because the colour 'red' is natural expression of the mutative principle (*rajas*). It is the outer expression of dynamism or activism. Thus, symbols are grounded in very basics of reality and enjoy the sanction of human psychic. In this sense 'symbol' are not invented but discovered. A symbol is ontologically rooted. For example, 'flame' is taken as the symbol of passion and 'River', as the symbol of transitoriness.

3.2.2. Symbol and Symbolised

The significance of '*Yantra*' in Tantra is of paramount importance. *Yantra* is the visual symbol having its impact on the mind. For example, when one concentrates on a triangle, mind becomes extroverted. When one ideates on a inverted triangle, mind becomes introverted. The former is the symbol of action (*karma*) and the latter, the symbol of knowledge (*jñana*). But when the inverse triangle is superimposed on the other, it takes mind to a state of equilibrium. Action demands that mind flows outward in order to attend to the various needs and duties. The external movement of the mind must be brought under control because if it is allowed to go unchecked, it (mind) is likely to crucify and degenerate. Obsession with externalities makes one forget the ultimate purpose. One mistakes the relative as absolute. Hence, there is need for constant remembrance of the 'goal'. This is possible only when mind becomes introversal. But if the mind is completely introverted one is likely to lose the capacity for adjustment with externalities. Hence, there is the need for two triangles, one being superimposed on the other. When knowledge and action are pursued with harmony, it gives rise to 'devotion' which is represented by the symbol 'rising sun'. As the Sun brings an end to the darkness of night, the psychic chamber of the individual is illumined by arousal of devotion. Symbols are evocative. They arouse subtler propensities in the mind and thereby drive the baser propensities by the backdoor. Symbols effect the transition from consciousness of the actual to the consciousness of the real. They help one find meaningful linkages between past and present and make momentous choices for the future. They help us reconcile our fragmented and piecemeal understanding of the world and experiences, therein. One understand the distinction between what is 'desired' and the 'desirable', 'sacred' and 'profane', 'good' and 'evil' and their place in the whole. When action is performed with knowledge and devotion one is sure to come out victorious. Victory is represented by the symbol '*swastik*'. '*Swastik*' in the socio-religious parlance, is taken as a sacred symbol, signifying fulfilment. But is spiritual domain, '*swastik*' symbolizes spiritual victory, victory of *avidya*, over '*vidya*', the 'good' over 'evil'.

Religious symbols are not amenable to literal interpretation. They get meaning from the socio-ethico-religious milieu. With change in the environment, religious symbols acquire newer significance. That explains why a symbol has a life-span. Some symbols acquire significance and go out of significance, with change in the mindset of the people or change in the environment. The real challenge before the theologian is to offer interpretation of 'symbol'. Religious men make use of concepts which have a definitive meaning in common parlance. When ordinary words are applied to God they undergo a semantic metamorphosis. There is either accretion or depletion of meaning in respect of the predicates ascribed to God. When the terms and categories of ordinary language prove to be inadequate, symbols are invoked. In religious discourse, often, symbols become the only figure of speech and semantic option.

'Signs' are consciously invented whereas 'symbols' are born or discovered. The meaning of a 'sign' is ascribed from without whereas the meaning of 'symbol' is inherent in its very nature. Since relation between 'sign' and the 'signified' is fixed by convention, a particular sign can be replaced by another. But one symbol cannot be substituted by another, at our sweet will for the simple reason that a 'symbol' grows out of the 'collective-unconscious' which is moulded by the inner and outer reality over aptly brings in the simile of 'participation' to elucidate the nature and function of religious symbol. Unlike a sign, symbol participates in its meaning. For example, national flag (symbol) participates in the power and dignity of a nation. Symbol evokes appropriate meaning and emotion in the individual and draws the mind to deeper recesses of reality and significance which remain otherwise unnoticed.

Religious symbols, in particular, stir the deeper cords of our being so that the mind, heart and soul are awakened to the very core of our being. In other words, it enables the individual to rediscover the reality in its depth-dimension which is otherwise termed as the 'transcendent', 'numinous' and 'holy'. Unlike 'signs' which are passive, religious symbols serve as active facilitators of thinking and decision making. They introduce us to broader canvas, deeper dimension and disclose new relations that are normal slurred over or ignored. Thereby, thy help the individual gain clarity make momentous existential choices with regard to oneself and in relation to others.

Since 'symbol' participates in the 'symbolized' it tends to replace that which it signifies. In other words, in course of time when a 'symbol' finds deeper root in human psyche, the semantic duality between the 'symbol' and the 'symbolized' tend to coalesce. A symbol replaces the symbolized and gets posited as the ultimate. There is progressive erosion of meaning leading to a total collapse. The signified (content) gets eclipsed in the symbol (form). For example, in all forms of idolatry, idol symbolizes an ideal. Here, the idol remains as a means to ideate on the ideal. Idol is the means (fulcrum) that helps the devotee to go beyond the finiteness of the 'idol' and establish oneself in the universality of the 'ideal'. As the devotee progresses, the idol thins into insignificance. Thus, idol serves as the ancillary device to realize the transcendent (infinite). Often, it so happens that the sacramental observances associated with idolatry, make one remember only the 'idol' (symbol) and forget the 'ideal'. This is what is termed as 'demonization of symbol'. Demonization is the reverse process of divinization wherein there is the death of the 'symbolized' in the 'symbol'. Symbols are discourse-specific and environment-specific. A symbol which is significant in one discourse or in a given circumstance, may have no meaning or have different meaning in a different sets of meaning in orthodox Hindu religion and in '*vidya tantra*'. Mecca may not have the same significance, in its depth-dimension, in a non-Islamic framework. That is why symbols remain immune to external criticism. Given the significance of the symbol in a given framework, all that one should attempt is to understand and interpret its meaning through intimate participation in the framework. Participation in a discourse again requires that one imbibes the on tic as well as the epistemic presuppositions, so that various interpretations of a symbol do not contradict but complement one another.

Symbols are inextricably bound up with fundamental cultural constructs. They draw our attention to deeper reaches of reality, thereby, urge the individuals to reset their priorities. They help us mend our myopic visions and narrow world-views which make us mistake the 'relative' as 'absolute', 'appearance' as 'reality'. Primary symbols in religion are those that stand out as central, focal and lend meaning to secondary symbols. Rites, rituals, prayers and observances center round these primary symbols the image of Buddha in Buddhism, Mecca in Islam, Cross in Christianity are primary symbols. The concepts and doctrines, principles and practices in a particular religion, derive their meaning from the primary symbols. Primary symbols need not necessarily be visual. A church bell, reading of *Namaj* by the mullah, *kiirtan* refines like *'Hare krsna Hare Ram'*, *'Baba Nam kevalam'*, *'Gayatri manra'*, cryptic cosmic refrains like *'Om tatsat'*, can be taken as non-visual symbols which ca up the whole web of meaning to the mind. There are some symbols which appear in different religious frameworks. But in such cases the same symbol acquires different world of meaning. Moon in Christianity is associated with Virgin Mary. In Islam, it is symbolic of the prophet moving from Mecca to Medina. In Chinese religion it is construed a abode of the celestial bodies. Thus, the significance of religious symbols is to be deciphered against the canvas of socio-cultural ambience and the collective psyche.[9]

Paul Tillich in his doctrine the 'symbolic' nature of religious language distinguishes the difference between a sign and a symbol. Both the terms point to something beyond themselves but a sign signifies that to which it points and a symbol participates in that to which it points. For instance a sign is like the traffic lights, the red light signifies that drivers are ordered to halt and the green light signifies to start and go on. A symbol on the other hand is like a national flag it signifies the dignity and power of a nation it represents. Symbols have an inner connection with the reality symbolized and grow out of the individual or collective unconscious and consequently have their own life span and decay. Unlike conventional signs, symbols open up levels of reality which otherwise are hidden from us. The clearest instance of this twofold function of symbols is provided by the arts which enable us to convey something of the beyond through symbols and at the same time opens us to new sensitivities and powers of appreciation in ourselves.

Tillich holds that there is only one literal, non-symbolic, statement that can be made about the ultimate reality which religion calls God. That statement is God is Being-itself, beyond this all theological statements such as, God is eternal, the creator, and loves his creation is symbolic. Religious faith according to him is the state of being 'ultimately concerned' about the ultimate and it can only express itself in symbolic language. Thus the language of faith is the language of symbols; in no other way can faith express itself adequately.

Any assertion about God must then be symbolic, in this manner God becomes a symbol. A symbolic expression is one whose proper meaning is negated by that to which it points, and at the same time it is also affirmed by it. This affirmation gives the symbolic expression a sufficient basis for pointing beyond itself. A concrete assertion of God uses a segment of finite experience in order to convey something about him even though it transcends the content of this segment and also includes it. The finite segment of experience then becomes the vehicle of a concrete assertion about God; it is affirmed and negated at the same time.

Tillich's writings on the whole are written in a way as to preserve the flexibility and ambiguity of his conception of the symbolic character of religious language. His writings can be developed in either of two opposite directions, negative and positive. I shall at this point consider his doctrine in its theistic development, in connection with the view of J.H. Randall and how it can also be developed naturalistically.

The negative aspect of Tillich's doctrine of religious symbols corresponds to the negative aspect of the doctrine of analogy. Tillich insists that we don't use language literally or univocally, when we speak of the ultimate reality because our terms are derived from our limited finite experiences and thus cannot be applied to God. When the word is used theologically its meaning is always partially negated by that to which it points. This doctrine constitutes a warning against thinking of God as though he were merely a vastly magnified human being (anthropomorphism). The alternative to this negative view is his theory of participation. Here he says that a symbol participates in the reality to which it points but fails to clarify the central notion of participation, according to him everything that exists participates in Being-itself. What then is the difference between symbols participating in Being-itself and the way in which everything else participates in it?

The application of Tillich's doctrine of participation to theological statements raises further questions. Complex theological statements have they emerged from the unconscious, whether individual or collective? How do these statements open up different levels of reality which are otherwise hidden from us in the depths of our being? These two characteristics of symbols seem to a great extent more applicable to the arts than to theological statements. Indeed this is the case; Tillich's tendency to incorporate aesthetic awareness to religion suggests the naturalistic development of his proposition.[10]

3.3. RELIGIOUS HERMENEUTICS

Language is the unique possession of man. It is the medium through which ideas, views, doctrines and experiences are shared with others and preserved for posterity. Human-beings think and feel alike. Meaning is the 'universal', expressed through different forms, in different ways. That is why it (meaning or idea) is shared by the members of a linguistic community. Individuals distanced by space and time, think alike, feel alike and respond alike to a stimuli. The points to the shared nature of human mind and understanding. Language is either spoken or written. In every speech situation, the speaker or writer intends to convey something to the hearer or reader through language. Thus, language, as such, is fraught with intentionality.

Every instance of successful speech is a case of 'encoding of meaning' through signs or symbols. Every instance of understanding is a case of decoding of meaning by the reader or hearer, as the case may be. A text is always context-specific. Meaning is not out there as the inalienable part of 'sign' or 'symbol'. 'Meaning' is something that accrues to the sign or symbol, on account of convention or socio-cultural ambience. In turn, convention is subject to the contingencies of physical, psychic and social environment which constitute the text. A text therefore, always smacks of situationally or historicity. Similarly, understanding involves interpretation. Here lies the significance of 'Hermeneutics' which concerns itself with the method of interpretation and understanding of texts, 'Hermeneutics' relates itself not only to the study of texts but also symbols and symbolic artefacts in form of art, sculptor, architecture.

'Hermeneutics' is derived from a Greek word, meaning 'an interpreter'. The term has its religious moorings in Greek Pantheon. Greek God 'herms' is depicted as one who used to interpret the message of regulations of God to the lesser mortals. Thus etymologically, 'hermeneutics' came to signify the process of understanding a text clearly.

'Hermeneutics' is a method of science of interpretation which appeared in form of literary hermeneutics, philosophical hermeneutics, and religious hermeneutics. Hermeneutics assumes added significance when one is concerned with interpretation of 'terms' and 'symbols' in a religious discourse. When expressions of everyday language are employed in religious discourse, their meaning gets transfigured. So, interpretation of a religious text becomes all the more challenging. Religious hermeneutics, primarily, focuses upon study of religious texts, symbols and artefacts.

Given the hermeneutical canvas, it is pertinent to reflect upon the nature of interpretation of religious texts. It provides a theoretical framework for understanding the nature of interpretation. Scriptural hermeneutics, as a special category of religious hermeneutics, is concerned with the system of interpreting religious texts. According to traditional scholars, "hermeneutics" involves a circular process. The meaning of parts i.e. words or sentences, become meaningful in their relation to the text as a whole. Similarly, the meaning of a text stands out in relation to the parts i.e. sentences and words. Thus, there is a circular movement from part to whole and whole to part. Thinkers like Dilthey and Schleimaker contend that a faithful understanding of a text can be had only by getting at the 'meaning' which the author intended to communicate. Interpretation is not an objective discovery of what is out there in the text. It involves creative reconstruction is as creative an act, as the creation of a text. Needless to say that both the author and the interpreter are subject to the contingencies of historicity or situationally. Man is a prisoner of time, place and tradition. That explains why the creation of a work of art, as much as its interpretation, smack of 'situationality'. Thus, there are two extreme views, one claiming that 'meaning' is out and our objective and impersonal, while others contend that 'meaning' is subjectively ascribed to the text. There are again others who subscribes to the thesis that 'meaning' is the outcome of the semantic interface between the historicity of the text and that of the interpreter.

Understanding involves interpretation. If 'interpretation' is a process, 'understanding' is the product. That which is available for interpretation is the 'as-structure. That which influences the interpretation is the 'fore-structure' which consists of pre-conceptions and pre-judgements. 'As-structure' let's itself to be seen or known through the 'fore-structure'. Even if the interpreter, somehow gets at the exact meaning which the author sought to convey, it is not an instance of replication but a case of self-understanding by the interpreter. It is as good as looking at an object by same kind of glasses from the same distance from the same perspective by different individuals. So, the perceived objectivity only tantamount to shared subjectivity. The 'subjectivisation of objectivity' is misconstrued by the traditional thinkers, as 'objectvisation of subjectivity. We are the carries of the legacy of our past but we are not tied to it. Rather, the past is created and recreated in us so that it serves as a fulcrum, a spring board that helps us to live unto future, in and through the present. Man is inherently finite in so far as he cannot transcend his situationally. Individuals belonging to the same tradition may differ with regard to the interpretation of the text because each individual is a unique subject in respect of his psychic make-up and situationally. Meaning of a text, therefore, goes beyond what the author intended to convey. In this sense, a text goes beyond the author. One can, therefore, say that understanding is not merely reproduction of the past but end result of the fusion of the situations of the text and that of the interpreter. Hermeneutic phenomenon rules out the exclusiveness of the subject (interpreter) and the object (text). It underlines the intimate semantic interface between the two. As a result, ontology gives way to epistemology. Assertor (apophantical) insight makes room for hermeneutical insight.

Understanding involves interpretation. It is true not only of understanding a text but also of any cognition whatsoever. Even a piece scientific knowledge, with its avowed ideal of getting at 'pure objective' is not free from hermeneutical bias. The framework of observation, observer-observed relationship has their influence on what is observed. The observer stands as a veritable hindrance in observation. Even our "existential awareness" is hermeneutical because the way the individual relates himself with his family, friends, and society, at large, depends upon his psychological make-up, value-awareness, pre-judgements etc. Every instance of our perception is hermeneutically tempered. The butterfly is not the same object for a child, a life-scientist, a poet and a spiritualist. It is not the same sea for a fisherman and a newlywed couple, a botanist and a hunter; It is also grossly mistaken to think that 'reason' has the unique capacity to arrive at 'objectivity'. If it is so, why do philosophers differ? Why is it that a foundational text in philosophy lends itself to varied interpretations? If the truth is one, why is it that scholars perceive it differently? If the Upanishads are said to contain the pristine metaphysical; truths, how is it that Shankar, Ramanuja and Madhava give us different accounts of them. Monism, dualism and Pluralism are but varied consequences of the philosopher's attempt to understand reality. Realism, idealism and phenomenalism are but three alternative accounts of the knowledge-phenomena.

Every cognitive enterprises, be it existential, scientific or philosophical, is hermeneutical. It is more pronounced in religious domain. Both the believer and non-believer live in the same world. The so-called virgin facts are same for both the theist and atheist. But the way they perceive, relate, and interpret things and events are radically different. The believer discovers 'divine will' behind everything that there is or happens. For the non-believer, things take place fortuitously, subject to the iron laws of causality. The former says, 'God is now here' and the latter says, 'God is nowhere'. The believer seeks to explain change teleological i.e. in terms of purpose (*telos*) and non-believer explain everything in terms of causal antecedent. Interestingly, the phenomenal world is made intelligible in both the ways though the adequacy of the either is put to test when one tries to understand the reality as a whole. This certainly goes to show that the world we live in is our own construction.

Religious thinker's mystics, intuitionists, vouchsafe for a state, whereof the exclusiveness of the subject and object is overcome. As a result, there remains no room for subjective interpretation of the objective. All that one is left with is an existential awareness, different from awareness of particulars which lend themselves to alternative interpretations. In other words, the highest state (transcendental stance) as envisaged by intuitionists, mystics is non-hermeneutical. Hermeneutical predicament is coeval with the existence of 'mind' and its functional expression in form of predication and interpretation.

Religious discourse is intimately bound up with hermeneutic understanding. The meaning of idioms and expressions largely depend upon what a religious follower understands by it. In the religious pronouncement, '*sarve bhavantu sukhinah*', the word '*sarve*' (all) has different meaning and appeal to different persons. For one, 'all' may mean 'all living beings', i.e. human fellows. It may mean 'all living beings' for one who carries the conviction that god is present in every living particular, tiny or big. For a realized one, 'all' means every expression, animate and inanimate. Similarly, in the commandment 'Love your neighbour as thyself', 'neighbour' may mean 'human neighbour' or it may mean every particular in the creation for a devout Christian who takes whole creation as the play of God and every particular as a living glory of God. Thus, the seminal concepts in religious texts lend themselves to different interpretations.

'Kuruksetra', in the Bhagavad Gita is taken by most of the Hindus as the place where the great war of Mahabharata was really fought. But a reflective follower of Hinduism finds added significance in it. For him, *'kuruksetra'* means the human body or the microcosm. The war is interpreted as the conflict between forces of 'good' and 'evil'. The fall of the *Kauravas* is interpreted as the eventual triumph of 'good' over 'evil'. Religious symbols carry different shades of significance to its followers depending on the degree of psychic maturation and spiritual elevation.

Though the symbol 'cross' (†) reminds one of the supreme sacrifice of the son of God, Jesus, the redeemer; its real import and impact on a devout Christian depends upon how far one has traversed on the God-ward path. What it did mean for the contemporaries, is vastly different from what it means to us today. Mere sight of the 'cross' may push an ardent follower to a state of trance whereas the 'cross' doesn't have such intense impact on an average church-goer for whom the 'cross' is a constant reminder of love and sacrifice which gives renewed inspiration to walk on the path of love and service by overcoming the lures of the world.

The 'swastik' is used in different religions and caries different significance for the followers. For Hindus, 'swastika' stands for everything auspicious and sacred. In *tantra*, 'swastika' is symbol of spiritual victory or final fulfilment. It is also part of *yantra (tantric form)* on which the spiritual practitioner has to ideate upon, resulting in active transmission of spiritual power into the practitioner. Similarly, the rituals and religious formalities have manifold significance, at least, the overt and covert meanings i.e. the surface and hermeneutical significance. The ritual of hurling stones at the pillars at Mina during Hajj has profound import for a conscious follower. Hurling stones means the determined effort to destroy or eradicate evil. The festival of colours (Holy) has deeper meaning than mere play with colours. The 'colour' (*varna*) doesn't mean external colour (physical colour) but the colour of the mind. As is the dominant psychic trait, so is the wavelength of mind and so is the colour of the mind. Depending on the basic disposition of mind, individuals are classified into four different categories. Colour is significative of imperfection, limitation or distortion. So, while offering colours to the Lord, the devotee prays, *O! God take away the colours of my mind* (my imperfections) and make me colourless (*avarna*). So, the festival of colours signifies man's eternal effort to move from imperfection to perfection, from the state of *varna* (being colored) to *avarna* (states of being decolored).

This, of course, should not make one construe that understanding is out and out subject-specific. Had it been so, one could not explain the commonalities of beliefs, practices, even shared convictions among the members of a religious community. This is because the worldview, ethics and practices, command unconditional allegiance of its followers. There is observed homogeneity in respect of how believers think, value and act, by and large. Needless to say that, the perceived commonality is the consequences of the fact that they share from common universals. Thus, it is not difficult to see that 'objectivity', pure and absolute, is a myth and misnomer. As long as there remains the duality of the subject and object i.e. as long as we find ourselves in the domain of the conceptual; every cognitive enterprise, be it literally, philosophical or religious, remains inherently bound up with the hermeneutical predicament. It is only by transcending 'mind', that one can reach a state which is 'trans-hermeneutical'.[11]

CHAPTER - 4
DIVERSITY OF RELIGIONS

A central question in contemporary philosophical activity regarding religious diversity. Whether religious diversity is a reason for questioning one's religious beliefs. The globalized world abounds in a plurality of religions, their beliefs and practices. Every day we hear about violence in the name of religion, great in a magnitude and impact which no other country and civilization have ever experienced. There are religious wars for dominating the planet, inhuman violence, and verbal assault. Religions now are creating more problems than solving them. In response, Tenzin Gyatso– the present Dalai Lama – has recently stated that interreligious harmony can be attained by understanding and appreciating other traditions inherent in them.[1]

The post-modern period, especially the last quarter of the 20th century has witnessed two different processes with contradictory, aspirations, emphasis, and demands. Globalization, with emphasizing global consciousness for constituting a global community, is on the rise. Simultaneously, there is an assertion of the ethno-religious identity across different parts of the world. Reconciling these two processes has become a global challenge. The earlier models and paradigms for solving the dilemma are being questioned The post-modern and post-colonial conditions appear incongruent with the Enlightenment projection of uniformity, homogeneity and universality based on reason and rationality for creating a harmonious universe. The post-modernist and post-colonial theory, philosophy and approaches have rejected the validity of the paradigm of modernity and the basic principles of modernism. Deconstruction of modernism has been substituted by great emphasis on multiplicity, heterogeneity, plurality, specificity, and diversity.

The nature, scope and significance of religion the individual and society have been speculated and for debated upon several centuries. The approaches to an understanding of religion – philosophical, theological, anthropological, sociological – and the related dimensions of religious ideas are quite ancient. The relation between religion and society has been very close; having wide, intricate elaborate and complex ramifications: The aim of religion is to provide spiritual and moral sustenance to individuals, the ethical codes of social life and moral order, regulating and creating cultural forms, for cohesion in society.

Globalization of religions in the past meant certain religions becoming global universal. But this is qualitatively different from what is understood today as "globalization". James Kurth in The Templeton Lecture on "Religion and World Affairs" describes "globalization" as steadily progressing process over time, spreading over space, and inevitable in its development. But globalization is also a world revolution disrupting the culture, traditions and customs of people, threatening their security, safety, and identity also.

Globalization is an important issue in the different intellectual and political agendas, posing important questions about what is regarded as the fundamental dynamic of our time a series of changes that is totally charging institutions, social and economic relations in the 21st century. Globalization is a political and imperialist project, which is using both science and religion in an irreconcilable way.

Since early 21st century practice of tolerance is in damage and religious diversity is a major cause of this problem. Since, the past two decades, diversity too has been debated upon by philosophers and theologians. What philosophers have found especially difficult in religious diversity is the epistemological problem it raises. Philosophers in their debates have focused mainly on the major world religions - Hinduism, Buddhism, Judaism, Christianity, and Islam. Although the philosophers did not discuss the concept of tolerance directly, there is a close relation between the epistemological problems generated by religious beliefs and the political problems resulting from religious diversity for e.g. Christianity. Natural theologies justify their belief in God through arguments for the existence of God. Christian religious experiences are another source of justification, spectacular experiences reported by the mystical virtuosi and the more mundane experiences of the ordinary Christians. A third justification is the divine revelation found in Christian canonical scripture. And, the fourth source for most Christians, is the authoritative teaching of a church believed to be guided by the Holy Spirit.

Before we judge and comment on the rational acceptability of that belief system, challenges to the Christian worldview must be considered, especially the existence of evil. The plurality of religions and their conflicting beliefs are another vexing challenge. And the increasing in religiously pluralistic societies, growth of global media, and transportation channels has made this challenge more salient in contemporary. Today, a Christian who is aware about religious diversity will understand that other world religions also have equally impressive sources of justification: They can put forward strong philosophical arguments for the basic concepts of their worldviews. They too are backed by rich experiential traditions. They also have authoritative institutions that texts and individuals teaching great lessons and paths to liberation from the ills miseries of human life. But, some distinct claims of the Christians, understood traditionally, contradict the core doctrines of other major religions. Though each religion is justified by its own sources, only one of them can be fully true. Therefore each religion is an unconquered enemy of the other religions. Religious diversity thus becomes the cause of the evils of intolerance. But it also promises a remedy for the very malady it has created.[5]

While discussing religion and globalization, we have to see whether globalization unites or divides religions; produces new-fangled religions; and is directly related to fundamentalism and religion based terrorism. It is also relevant to check whether for its new imperialist project, globalization is exploiting different religious forms; whether fundamentalism and religion-inspired terrorism have grown since the beginning of globalization; and whether religions, instead of being traditional belief systems, have developed new dimensions far removed from the spiritual and religious realms.[6]

The concept and discussion of pluralism in post-modernism, deviates from the context of collective aspect of experience and sharing. The post-modernist obsession with autonomous individual, individuality of identity, rejection of universal, and emphasis on particular-specific, challenge to Enlightenment project, redefinition of reason, rationality and scientism results in a kind of circular causality, wherein the reconciliation between individual identity and collective requires, individual aspirations and common good appear as an endless process. Recognition and pronouncement of pluralism is, a major concern of post-modernism, but in effect it has no rational limit. The creative tension resulting from this predicament requires an alternative model and a paradigm for mediating between the individual and the collective, the particular and universal and for blending different socio-cultural identities and patterns.

Pluralism basically denotes the existence of many of modes and methods, thoughts and ideas, political and culture forms, and plurality of identities. It is deconstructs all form of monism and uniformity. In the context of social relationships, principles and political forms, pluralism appeals to pluralistic society. But, the meaning and context of pluralism have not been uniform in its course of development. With changing emphasis and focus, as a concept, pluralism has been conceptualized, articulated and used differently in contemporary times, especially in the context of post-colonialism and post-modernism.

Pluralism, amongst other things signifies: a humble and relativistic admittance that there is a spectrum of cultural values; resistance to all forms of cultural imperialism; freedom from rationalism and Enlightenment scientism; fruitful methodological diversity; acceptance of varied ways of being and knowing; openness and creativity in theory; and comprehending a vast range of social interests and interest groups in the modern political scenario, acknowledging democracy as an end in itself; awareness of the complexities of political affiliations; the notion that our political and social identities are chosen and not inherited; anti-utopian political horizons; enshrinement of the principle of different but equal.[2]

India is a pluralistic society both in its content and form. The coexistence of diverse identities based on language, ethnic formation, religion and caste is a characteristic of that plurality. This plurality characterizes a unique harmony between different identities on the one hand, and with multi-faceted, multi-form, multi-layered common social identity, on the other. A sense of common identity marks the content of Indian pluralism and provides a context for social expression. It is this content which has provided internal strength to the continuity of India as a distinct civilization which is not an exclusive preserve of any caste, religion, ethnic or regional group, language. Exclusive ideology of restricting the composite heritage of India to any of its layers or forms is hierarchical, hegemonic and homogeneous in spirit.

The resurfacing of religious exclusivism is challenged by the existential reality of India. The coexistence of major world-religions: Hinduism, Christianity, Islam, Buddhism and Judaism; in addition to the animistic religions of the native population is important indicator in this regard. Each of these religions has its own codes of conduct, doctrinal principles and claims of superiority and inferiority, modes of worship, falsity and truth, and own parameters of evaluation. In spite of the apparent differences and antagonistic doctrines, there are underlying principles promoting mutual recognition, respect and tolerance; and in some cases sharing and mutual acceptance are a part of collective life and collective experience. The Bhakti traditions of Hinduism; Sufism in Islam; and Sikhism propounded by Guru Nanak, greatly illustrate this aspect of collective experience and pluralistic principles of accommodation and social interaction. This has facilitated the development of a syncretic tradition and composite culture encompassing the spirit of humanism – a sea bed of accommodation in reality!

Religious pluralism as a fact of and an ideological foundation of Indian social life is widely known. This reality has been recognized by the leaders of the Indian National Movement, and enshrined in the Constitution of India by the founding fathers. Different religious communities enjoy exclusive rights for self-expression together with the rights of liberty and equality. For the preservation and protection of communities, their distinctness, cultural identity and religion, different institutional mechanisms have been created outside and within the Constitution. The extent to which these mechanisms and provisions are effective is a matter for debate and critical examination. But one feature which is largely recognized is that India in its federal document, i.e. the Constitution, promises the promotion and protection of different religious communities. It regard it is important to note that the idea of religious pluralism is not limited merely to inter-religions. There is ample scope and instances of intra-religious pluralism also which defy all claims and attempts of monolithic construction of any exclusive religious community, though the degree, extent and degree of plurality differ from religion to religion due to its own historicity and context. [3]

During the freedom movement and framing of the Constitution independent India was never expected to be a theocratic state. Even Mahatma Gandhi, a pious Hindu, considered religion as a private affair. The Constituent Assembly and the Constitution framed by it delegated religion to the private domain of the individual, without in anyway interfering even with the issue of religious conversions lately has acquired great political significance and has been dragged into the public domain. The extent do which religion found a place in the Constitution was only for rectifying certain historically situated, socially and politically debilitating, for disharmony, deleterious and dysfunctional accretions, anomalies, and malignancies, and to gradually creating a harmonious society.

A hundred years ago, Swami Vivekananda stated that although religion has been a great blessing to humankind; it has at the same time; it has contributed much to horror than religion. Religion has bestowed peace and love and also aggressive hatred. It has bred not only brotherhood between human beings but has also generated bitter enmity between them. While religion has provided charitable institutions, hospitals for (wo)men and even animals, it has also flooded the world with blood. It is evident however, that diversity by itself is not enough to justify religious conflicts, because history has shown that people belonging to different religion, origin, creed, color, have coexisted harmoniously. All religious conflicts arise from two causes: (i) intrinsic and (ii) external.

Intrinsic cause pertains tenets, customs, or doctrines of one religion which are totally opposed to another religion. External cause is manipulation of religion by the state supposed institutions have done by manipulating religion institutions, political parties, vested interests, etc. commenting on the damage by manipulating religion. Swami Vivekananda says that religion should the evils and violence religion not be blamed for because there are not the faults of religion. No religion persecuted human beings burnt witches. The harm was done by Politics in the name of religion. A study of the history of religious conflicts reveals that the nature and character of the conflicts have undergone various changes and resulted in disastrous consequences that are totally despicable and abhorrent. These changes are due to the relation between religion and human beings in the 18th century; known as the age of Enlightenment, which climaxed in anthropocentrism, humankind got enthroned, and God was dethroned, with this astonishing through the supersession of the Mediaeval Theo-centric model. Human beings became the sole arbiters of the cosmos, equipped with agency, self-determination, and autonomy. As a result of this religion and its dogmas became regarded as obstacles in the path of human progress, control and prosperity. Looking back we can see that before the eighteenth century religions were concerned with salvation. Many non-secular battles and persecutions of the middle Ages were concerned with hell and heaven universal dominion having some dogma as a weapon. Revolutionary secularization of religion that started with the French Revolution, and Industrial Revolution helped religion become more related with human concerns. Consequently, religious disagreements are not doctrinal differences, but disagreements about economic, political, and social problems.

India is a land of racial harmony, inclusivism and cultural pluralism from ancient times until now. Indian ethos is based on freedom, toleration, harmony and openness. But since recent times communal disturbances, destruction of places of worship, and killing religious leaders, have become common affairs. Another major problem is the growth of fundamentalism. These occurrences are detrimental to and deviations from the Indian ethos. Moreover, these are Indian responses to aspects antagonistic to its ethos. Since communal and religious disharmony has increased both in India and abroad, religious harmony has become very important and essential for everybody.[2]

Major world religions like Hinduism, Christianity, Islam, Judaism and Buddhism have been discussed in the earlier Chapters, summarizing their basic tenets and common features. Judaism, Christianity, and Islam are monotheistic religions agree that God; a personal and perfect, who has created the cosmos according to His divine purpose and that it has a telos. But this analysis of God, and postulations affirming or negating His existence, has overlooked many differences and subtleties distinguishing Judaism, Christianity, and Islam., it has even ignored some conceptual differences regarding the nature of the theistic God – for instances, Christianity, proclaims God is a trinity and that the logos assuming a human form incarnated in flesh and in a unique way as the Jesus of Nazareth – this view is not acceptable to which Judaism and Islam. The Eastern religions - Hinduism and Buddhism, also depart in their theistic interpretation of the ultimate. We have to take into consideration the significant differences between these religions and question whether these different religions are true. It appears that they all cannot be true. Therefore, we have to see how a person who belongs to one religion views or should view other religions.

Theism is not restricted merely to Judaism, Christianity and Islam for instances, those people who worship Lord Vishnu and Lord Siva in Hinduism, also belong within the theistic traditions called Vaishnavism and Saivism. The *Bhagvad-Gita* or the (Song of the Lord) is a dialogue between Lord Kṛṣṇa and Arjuna, on the battle field of Kurukshetra. It expounds the path of devotion (*bhakti-mārga*) as the easiest and best means to attain liberation (*mokṣa*) through the desire less performance of selfless- actions (*niskāma-karma*). But ancient literature of the Hinduism, the *Upaniṣads*, teach that the ultimate Reality, is impersonal and that liberation from the cycle of rebirth occurs when the individual soul experiential knowledge of Brahman –Ātman identity. *Advaita Vedanta* declares that Brahman is changeless, actionless, infinite, attributeless, fullness, and one only without a second (*ekam eva advitiyam*). The philosophy of Advaita can be summaraized as- "*Brahman satyam jagat mithyā, jivo Brahmaiva nā parah.*" which means that Brahman alone is real, the world is illusory, and the soul/*jīva*/is no other than Brahman. The universe of material phenomena and individuals are illusory. Liberation involves realizing one's essential identity with Brahman.[3]

Therefore, as mentioned earlier there are great differences prevailing between the major religious of the world. The first difference is concerned with the interpretation of the ultimate Reality an impersonal Absolute personal God. The second difference involves of issues about our empirical life and final destiny. It discusses whether there is a cycle of birth and death, and transmigration and reincarnation survive bodily death and reappear on earth as soul in animal and human bodies as admitted in Eastern religions and denied by Western Thought. Does the ultimate human destiny involve merger of individual consciousness in the finitude of being? Or continuation as different individuals having unique experiences and thinking after union with the Divine? The third difference discusses the locus of revelation. Judaism recognizes the *Torah* as the locus of God's revelations, Christianity, declares Jesus as God, a view which both by Judaism and Islam reject Hinduism admits and promises incarnations/descents/*avataras* of the Divine in different forms. Then finally, there are different views about: (a) the existential predicament of human beings, (b) the paths to overcome the human predicament, and (c) the nature of salvation liberation Christianity, postulates that every human being inherits the original sin resulting from willful disobedience of God's command by Adam and Eve. Himself as Jesus Christ suffered to alone for our sin and facilitate our salvation, thereby saving Christians from eternal damnation. For attaining salvation, one must accept God's grace. This acceptance will ensure a relation of obedience to and love for Jesus - the Jesus Saviour. Thus saved, after death one attains eternal life and fellowship with God. According to *Advaita Vedanta* a system of in Indian philosophy, human birth is result from ignorance (*avidyā*) than from willful sinful actions. The material phenomena world is an illusory projection of *māyā*, and one's liberation from rebirth involves not securing another life fellowship with a personal God, but realizing one's identity with the ultimate reality Brahman. This can be actualized only when one pursues and practices these two kinds of knowledge (1) this I am not (*na aham idam*); and (2) This is not mine (*na-mama-idam*). Thereafter, by abandoning one's individual identity through union with the universal consciousness bereft of all difference and content one attains liberation, as declared by major text (*mahāvākya*) –That thou art (*tat tvam asi*).[4]

This Chapter will examine the issue of how one should understand and interpret the claims proffered by diverse religious regarding Reality and our position therein. Philosopher of Keith Yandell religion states that…religions make claims, because in the absence of assertions, religions will cease to be religions. Every religion posits a unique prognosis, eschatology and soteriology. Every religion examines human condition, and predicaments to provide a practical means to overcome them. All problems cannot arise from the same situation, and there is no one solution to all problems. Therefore, it is very important for us to describe the situation and the problem for one's salvation/liberation. What/who we are and what we have to be saved from have to be clarified. Hence, accepting a religion indicates admitting the inter-connection between situations, the issues and their solutions.[5] Not tolerating religions other than one's own results in conflicts and fundamentalism. Several factors influence one's attitude towards other religions. Four major inter-religious attitudes have been identified by Western follows: Exclusivism, Inclusivism, Pluralism and Relativism.

4.1. RELIGIOUS EXCLUSIVISM

Exclusivism affairs that only *one's own religion alone is true and that all other religions are false*. This view teaches that there can be only one way to salvation and one true revelation. It existed the West until the World Parliament of Religions conducted in Chicago in 1893. Even now, some religions and groups hold this view expressed in the Christian dogma as: "*Extra ecclesiam nulla salus*," means that there is no salvation. When exclusivism is aggressively expressed socially, it becomes which assumes violent and fundamentalism. The growth of fundamentalism in many religions, and the use of extremist and terrorist tactics by some fundamentalists pose great threat to global friendship, prosperity and peace in the contemporary world.[6]

Many have accepted Hick's pluralistic vision. But, thinkers like Alvin Plantinga and William Alston, have criticized Hick's views and supported a more exclusivistic approach. Defending exclusivism, Plantinga says that exclusivism involves the concepts or tenets of one religion, for e.g. Christianity claims that they are true and other religious beliefs that are not compatible with these tenets are false. The exclusivistic position and the pluralistic position, diametrically to one another. Therefore, denial that Hick's claim a religion cannot out comes into denial that any religion could provide tenets or forward concepts that exactly describe Reality gets falsified. Moreover, if the religious tenets claimed that all are not equally effective paths to Reality, Hick gets refuted Plantinga, claims that ethically or epistemically, a thinker cannot be criticized as inconsistent for advocating exclusivism because entertaining exclusivistic beliefs owes not mean that one is irrational, immoral, or unjustified.[7]

As a requisite, a good theory, the hypothesis is conservative in that it retains much of the past, present and relevant beliefs. Therefore, according to this view, since pluralism has novelty, it is not as conservative as exclusivism. Pluralism has a novelty only in the confines of the Abrahamic religions. In the case of Indian religions, it loses novelty, for example Nanak and Kabir and other pluralist thinkers of that period; and even earlier if we consider Asoka, and the heterodox systems in Islam, we can see Rumi, Al'Arabi and Al'Hallaj as examples. Pluralism is conservative in the sense that it begins with religions as they are for providing data for explanation. But it has novelty (in the West) when it explains conservation, continuity, and novelty are required in religion - otherwise the Church would have shrouded by mediaeval darkness. He then states that an exclusivist theory of religious diversity possesses these virtues. But since he did not explain the exclusivist theory of religious diversity, it becomes greatly difficult to comment on it. He states that he does question some, exclusivistic models which are conservative and also internally consistent. But, he has not shown what an 'exclusivistic models is. It is possible for theories to be highly conservative, and internally consistent by their very formation. But problems arise when we check whether they are externally consistent with regard to historical facts and the phenomenology of religions. And till Meeker formulates the theory which he has in mind, all claims about its virtues remains empty. He argues that 'Hick supports a broad pluralism and a also self-evident moral criterion which can undermine his pluralism. He says that for Hick the major religions of the world consider altruism as constitutive of liberation/salvation; and views his stand as founded on altruism as the heart of religion. But, there is a big misunderstanding because it rejects the crucial aspect of transcendence. Meeker's interpretation of salvation suggest transformation of human life from self-centredness to Reality-centredness, i.e. by reorienting a self-centric individual towards the Divine Reality. But this stipulative definition presupposes the postulated Real. The hypothesis of pluralism for Liberation/Salvation demands a through reorientation, from one's interest self-centeredness to a new transcendent Real, conceived and experienced as Shiva Vishnu, the Holy Trinity, Allah, the Tao, Brahman or the Dharmakaya. This liberating reorientation can be observed only through its results in human life. This, thus constitutes the criterion for evaluating, the authenticity of the individual, the religion and the historical tradition.

Among individuals, the fruits of liberation/salvation are very prominent in the "saints" not those designated by the Church (even though it includes some of them), but the laity. And, when we examine their lives, we can see that some of them have progressed greatly and transcended the ego, and their views about God, Dharma. Although traditional hagiographies are highly unreliable, they are often valuable, when it especially when they provide first-hand knowledge of spiritual personalities. Hence, the reason when we often hear that one living saint is more worthier than ten dead ones. The core of religion involves embracing the Real, the Ultimate Reality, and the Transcendent. This is further revealed by a transformed life full of compassion and love for others, sometimes for perverse actions. (Transcendence of the ego in dedication to hatred of others, as in absolute commitment to the Fuhrer and his Nazi ideology, thus rules itself out.

According to Meeker all the great faiths of the world admit. The ideal in Christianity is St. Paul's apostolic state. His statement that it is not he who lives, but Christ who lives in him, and that one should love one's neighbor is major tenets of Christianity. Islam, declares that a follower of God should totally surrender to God and His will oneself abandon one's self-will and reverse God in all walks of life. Every Sura of the *Quran* that God is merciful and gracious. The followers of Judaism have dedicated themselves to the religious tradition of the Hebrew for experiencing the God's hand. The *Talmud* declares that the whole of the Torah is based on the view that one should not do to another what is hateful to oneself. According to Buddhism, an individual has to abandon belief in the existence of an immutable eternal self for attaining enlightment characterized by loving kindness (*matta*) and universal compassion (*Karuṇa*) for all phenomena. Hinduism is not an "ism" involving strict codes and rigid dogmas but only a conventional name for diverse forms of Indian philosophical and rigorous thought and practices. Self-realization and though expression of Self-Brahman identity is the philosophy of Advaita, a popular school of Indian philosophy. Selfless devotion to God, fructifies when one refrains from worldly actions or remaining engaged in the world, practicing virtues and non-violence (*ahimsā*). A major ideal is that an individual should not do to another that which one considers as injurious to oneself. This, in short explains the rule of righteousness (*dharma*).

Meeker rightly states that the essence of morality involves not harming others but practicing loving compassion towards them which is self-evident to everybody except the psychopaths. Meeker interprets the self-evident of Plantinga as a foundational irrefutable belief, that cannot be proved, because it is fundamentally rooted in natural and human moral insight. This is what is taught by all world religions. But this does not mean that all the followers of a religion are living examples, or vitiate the view that saints and sinners are a plenty across the globe. For Meeker, the followers of one are not morally and spiritually better human beings than those of the other religions. Because, if this view is true, then, the exclusivist claim of a particular religion will get validated. Summarizing his objections,

Meeker states his dilemma, that "Hick should either (1) adhere to his ethical criterion and admit that all major religions do not measure up. But this position will affect his pluralism. Or, (2) he can abandon his 'self-evident' criterion. But this alternative will not have resources to strengthen his refutation of "selfish religions". In fact, all the religions abound in selfish people. But by "selfish religion" Meeker means the lack of altruism as the only constituent for salvation. There are scriptural texts in every religion that do not "measure up". For example, the *Bhagavad Gita* (where Kṛṣṇa participate in the battle), the Torah, the *Quran*, and the *New Testament*. Meeker upholds that Hinduism teaches the path of knowledge and also selfless action. The path of knowledge involves love and compassion. The Advaitic *jivanmukta* merged in Brahman, is calm like a flame when its fuel has been exhausted, and is consumed, an ocean of love without any, ulterior motive. But Meeker declares that altruistic behavior is not constitutive of liberation/salvation; or, that for Buddhism, it is sufficient for enlightenment. A through reorientation towards the Ultimate is a characteristic of liberation/Salvation and altruistic attitude is its natural fruit and insignia.

Meeker argues that Hick's conception of Buddhism and also forms of Hinduism undermines its position as a redemptive aspect of efficacious religion. His supposition is that only the elite are eligible for liberation in Buddhism and some systems of Hinduism. His claim would have been valid if he had admitted that these religions are liable to misinterpretation in this way. Because, as stated by him, this may not be the pure and normative interpretation of Buddhism which has enabled it become a great religion of the world. Buddhism teaches that life is full of misery, pain, and suffering, and recommends a path to terminate all human suffering. The path to liberation is for all and not merely a select few. Regarding Advaita and Hinduism referred to by him, it is exalted states of experience which can be attained in this life itself provide the seeker qualifies and is eligible for it. Liberation is open to everybody. All religions, including Christianity are vulnerable to misinterpretation in diverse ways. In his argument, Meeker commits two mistakes: (1) treating exclusivism as a theory without stating anywhere what that theory is like for explaining diversity and plurality; (2) criticize another for holding a position which one does not advocate – the view that altruism constitutes it as not consistent with pluralism. [8]

It is natural for a follower of a religion to that one's religion alone is true, and that the other religions are false. This happens because for the follower of a religion its basic claims are true. For e.g., if one believes that one goes to Heaven or Hell, according to one's actions after death; a person cannot at the same time admit the Buddhist and Hindu view that there is reincarnation after death. Therefore, exclusivism is right to an extent. Every religion professes a path to liberation/salvation from human misery. This is very significant and important for religion because a religion is not a mere aggregate of doctrines. The next question which arises now is how a particular follower of one religion views the prospects of another who adhere to a different religion. This question answered to some extent by the religion which one pursues because each religion claims that it alone is the path to liberation/salvation and that their religions too are paths to liberation or remain silent about it. A religion is exclusive it if claims that it alone confers liberation, and the others who do not follower of that religion will think that one's religion is true and that the others are false until one deviates from such a religion or view. It is very easy to comprehend how a exclusivism arises in religion (1) Initially, when religion arose, people did not know much about other faiths, cultures, paths to liberation, or religions. (2) The advent of monotheism resulted in the one God as omnipresent, omnipotent creator, controller and destroyer of the cosmos, and that one has to love God to attain liberation/salvation. Therefore, a follower of one religion believed that religion alone for attaining union with God. This attitude made orthodox Christianity a strong exclusivistic religion as seen among the Roman Catholics and Protestants. The council of Florence (1438-1445) declares that not just the Catholic, but also pagans, Jews heretics and schismatic can attain eternal life; if, before they died they joined the Church. Otherwise, they will have to go to the eternal fire prepared for the devil and his assistants.

The Catholic faith declares that salvation is impossible outside the Church. This was strengthened by a powerful missionary of Protestants in the 19th century. Indoctrination is an extension of the concept that there is salvation for all in the world. But there are difficulties in religions exclusivism. The practical difficulty is that millions of people belonging to other religious and cultures live and die without even knowing about salvation as taught by a particular exclusivistic religion.

As a Christian, John Hick a contemporary philosopher of religion puts the point this way: Christianity, God posits universal love. Salvation is the *summum bonum* willed by God for all (wo)men. After creating the whole of creation, God created man in his own image. But, paradoxically, the Christian way is the only path to salvation. A major section of humanity who have lived and died until now, were not Christians. If this is the Christians stand then how can the view that God is love and that He desires the salvation of all human beings accepted because then only a sections of humankind will be eligible for salvation.

Another problem for an exclusivist religion results from association with and the influence of other religions, the lives of their saints and founders who serve as ethical role-models and are paragons of devotion. For example, It would be absurd and a naive idea if we say after knowing about the life and works of Gandhi and Hinduism that Mahatma Gandhi will go to hell because he did not convert to Christianity or any other exclusivist religion.[9]

4.2. RELIGIOUS INCLUSIVISM

Inclusivism arises when we consider the truth and discussed salvation in other religions but understand them as forms of truth and salvation discussed in one's own religion. Inclusivism maintains that *one's own religion alone is true, but does not reject other religions as false, because they are all embedded in one's own religion.* For inclusivism the revelation of one's own religion as perfect, final and fulfilling, whereas those other as religions are imperfect, preliminary and partial. Some aspects of Inclusivism can be seen in all the great world religions. Sri Kṛṣṇa's declaration in the *Bhagavad Gita*, 'In whatever way that in an individual chooses to attain Him, He blesses one in that way, "people everywhere follow my path', is cited often as an instance of Inclusivism among the Hindus. St. Augustine's statement in the 4th century anticipates inclusivism in Christianity. 'For example, the religion presently known as Christianity existed among the early people, until the time Christ's advent in the flesh, but it was not absent from the beginning of humankind. Therefore, the true religion which was already existent came to be known as Christian. In 1961, Karl Rahner German Catholic theologian was the first formulated, inclusivism as an inter-religious attitude. Karl Rahner viewed all religions as manifestation of Christ's life and His works. And those who worshiped Christ through diverse sacraments and rituals of other religions ignorant about this fact were called as 'anonymous Christians' by Rahner.

When Swami Vivekananda, says the concept of inclusivity par excellence, can be seen that the whole of religion contained in three variants Vedanta – Advaita, Visistadvaita, and Dvaita. But, later on Vivekananda used the term "Vedanta" in a very broad sense. Therefore, hence he cannot be regarded as advocating Inclusivism. [10]

The conception of inclusivity in Christianity implies that the Christianity is the only means to salvation, and that salvation is impossible for anybody without the activity of the Divine of that religion. But the inclusivity of Christianity negates difficulties associated with exclusivism by admitting that the Christian means to salvation includes means for those who, have no normal means of salvation since they belong to different times and places due to which for no fault of their, Christs gospel unavailable to them. In this way by rejecting the validity of other religions, Christian inclusivity permits the follower of other religions to attain salvation by pursuing the paths their religions. They can attain salvation by doing their best with a desire to obey the will of the Christianity God. Another alternative is to state that those who, due to no fault of theirs did not have an opportunity in this life to respond to Christ's gospel will have a chance to do it in the future world. These amendments enable the exclusivist aspects of a religion can be altered in favor of inclusivism.[11]

4.3. RELIGIOUS PLURALISM

Religious plurality and the interpretation of it are important issues debated in contemporary theology and philosophy of religion The *Weltanschauung* Religious pluralism declares that all the great world religions of the world are equal when we consider the question of salvation and truth. It also states that no religion is superior to another religion or make normative claim over other religion. Pluralism declares that all the religions of the world are true; there are many revelations and diverse paths to liberation/salvation. According to pluralism, human thought can envisage truth in multifarious forms. All religions are different soteriological spaces, through which humankind seeks salvation, according to John Hick. Pluralism attempts to promote understanding and harmony between religions without destroying the subtle differences between them. Pluralism can be appreciated only after we distinguish it from

Inclusivism and relativism because these two are diametrically opposed views. Pluralism admits that religions are different. Therefore, it recognizes their dignity, validity, and autonomy. For James Michael Lee, maintains that pluralism is not a cauldron in which we can dissolve all religions dissolve into one mass. Instead, real religious pluralism is like a mosaic wherein all religions are accorded autonomy, interactive and privileged positions that disclose the full reality of God better than anyone religion. But, this does not mean that the truths of diverse religions are relative and incompatible, and prevent the possibility of absolute truth. Because without Reality or absolute truth, every religion will get separated and become islands; thereby, preventing any interaction between them. For Professor Grant S. Shockley, pluralism is a methodical analysis of analysis facilitating objectivity, focus and critical evaluation. Universal and exclusive revelations and absolutes are valid, both in themselves, and for those who believe them. But, there are features of a greater truth described as unknowable by an individual. But, pluralism is not merely a theological matter because it is concerned more with practical issues than theoretical ones. Shockley upholds that essentially pluralism seeks a more ample functional interpretation of the meaning and nature of religion or theology, its place in diversity - racial, ethnic, linguistic and cultural. It also seeks ways to help people creatively in and coexist meaningfully amidst diversity; and corporately creates means for accomplishing common goals. Arnold Toynbee, W. E. Hocking, and Ernst Troeltsch, introduced in western philosophy the concept of religious pluralism Paul Tillich, Wilfred Cantwell Smith and John Hick Consolidated it further. And, John Hick's significant role in contemporary pluralist movement of the West needs mention. Hick calls his pluralist scheme as "Copernican revolution". He admits that the our faiths are God-centric: in that God is like the sun, the origin and source of light and life. His statement shows clearly a rejection of exclusive claims of religion. James Michael Lee a Professor in the University of Alabama has put forward eight 'Basic Principles of Religious Pluralism' as given below in an abridged and adapted form:

- The ultimate Reality is inexplicable. It is the primal source of all mysteries. In different religions, it expresses itself through revelations.
- Every religion is a unique social response and an attempt to accomplish to divine revelation.

- Every religious person regards of one's socio-cultural milieu interacts with God in unique diverse ways.
- As far as religious views are concerned, the follower of all religions as equally, but this does not mean the equality of all religions.
- It is very important to understand the principle and praxis of other religions.
- All attempts during comparison must take into consideration the views of that religion to ensure that comparisons are not invidious.
- Free discussion through dialogue between the followers of diverse religions will strengthen the value of comparisons.
- The follower of a religion should imbibe the beneficial and noble principles of other religions, for one's spiritual enrichment. The above mentioned aspect indicates the main trends in pluralism among contemporary western theologians. In this context, we have to pay attention to three more points.

(a) Pluralism is a general concern of all human beings and not an exclusive concern of the Church alone. Varied reasons as follows: (1) the wide spread social revolution of the 60's which took place in Europe and America; (2) the advent and influence of oriental ideas and spiritual leaders; (3) the great upheaval that resulted from a secularization of the religions and moral authorities. This liberated people from the stranglehold of institutionalized religion and (4) the co-existence of diverse ethnicities, initiated a multi-cultural awareness influencing the society as a whole, and reinforced the need for pluralism.

(b) But the above mentioned events have not reduced the ongoing debates on religious pluralism, because the attitude of people is greatly determined by education. Therefore, pluralism has come to the pedagogues, religious leaders and governments. Moreover, pluralism has become popular because it is a powerful and perfect antidote for the universal terror caused by Fundamentalism,

(c) Pluralism as discussed above is mainly based on Western premises and *Weltanschauung*. Therefore, it is not relevant and significant in the Indian context.[11]

John Hick advocates an admirable approach to religious pluralism. Supporting a plurality in the means to salvation, he observes that every world religions proffers such a path. He rejects the atheistic view about religion as a form of anthropomorphism. Employing the Kantian dichotomy of (1) noumena (things in themselves) (2) phenomena (things experienced through the categories of mind) he argues that one's descriptions and experiences are determined by the categories of comprehension and understanding of interpretations. Therefore, some understand the Ultimate Real through theistic concepts e.g. as Yahweh or Allah; whereas the others engage in pantheistic and impersonal ways (e.g. as *nirguṇa Brahman*). But, there still may be others who use a totally non-personal way (e.g. as Tao or *nirvana*). The Indian parable of the elephant and blind men illustrates this point, as for Hick, in our quest for the Real we are similar to the blind men –our viewpoints and claims are influenced and limited by the concepts of our culture and customs.

In his famous work, *An Interpretation of Religion*, Hick uses these differences and favours a pluralistic hypothesis:

He declares that there is an ultimate reality, which he calls as the Real. This Real is Trans-categorical (ineffable) and beyond the scope of the conceptual systems. But, its universal presence is experienced by human beings through various forms facilitated and mediated by our conceptual-linguistic systems and spiritual praxis.

For Hick although religious dogmas and doctrines are important personal transformation that occurs in an individual through religion is of great importance. He observes that the great religions of the world embody diverse conceptions and perceptions of, and correspondingly varying responses to the inner Real; and that through these religions the transformation of human beings from self-centeredness to Reality-centeredness and from non-saints to saints is getting actualized.

Hick uses several analogies for communicating the diverse aspects of religion and pluralist hypothesis. A very interesting one is the Wittgenstein's duck-rabbit picture which is a puzzle illustrating the dependence of ambiguity on cultural-formation; i.e. a culture which is not familiar with rabbits because it has only ducks. Hick uses the example to explain that the real is beyond scope of human understanding and that it can only be experienced authentically as Allah, Yahweh, Tao, Shiva, or Vishnu, depending on one's religion and the individual's experience of Reality. [12]

For Hick, no religion is superior to another because all of them are at par with one another. All great religions convey knowledge about the Real, provide a stereological goal for human pursuit and recommend the best means for its attainment. But the problem begins here. The pluralistic hypotheses that the Real is experienced validly through all the religions, and that they all proffer a stereological goal appears to be self-contradictory because while asserting all religious views regarding the Real and the stereological goal are equally true, Hick asserts that his own view is superior to and truer than all the other views.

In answer to the above criticism, we can show that the pluralistic hypothesis is a meta-theory, because it is an evaluatory theory of religions and not a mere hypothesis. Therefore, it is free from logical inconsistency.

There is another objection to the pluralistic hypothesis about the Real, resulting from the stand that all religious truth claims are contextual and perspectival. Moreover, the view that it is not about the noumena but about phenomena results in an epistemological problem leading to skepticism or agnosticism about the Real. Because if we cannot speak about the real, and posit attributes to it as being all-powerful, good, loving, non-dual, just, or impersonal, etc., because it is ineffable and, therefore, beyond human understanding, then, it becomes difficult to distinguish the Real as to whether it is merely a human mental projection or wish fulfillment?

Hick's Kantian response, to this criticism is based on his conception of the need for postulating an objective Real to account for various transformations and experiences in the historically rich religious traditions. But the difficulty for Hick is due to his interpretation of the Real as beyond characterizations and "neither personal nor non-personal". It makes one wonder how that "ineffable" category can lead to a moral or personal transfiguration so characteristic of Hick's position.

Another form of pluralism tries to avoid its philosophical problems. For example, aspectual pluralism, admits that there an ultimate objective Reality and that it is knowable. In a non-Kantian manner, they also state that the noumenon is attributable. Peter Byrne emphasizes this fact and who maintains, that different religions reflect complementary aspects of the Real. Different religious describe the one and the same Reality because it has varied aspect and the one transcendent expresses itself in different ways. The Real reveals it different aspects and differs according to diverse conceptual schema, praxis and religious structures.

The problem with view is that it comprehends only a part of the whole. Therefore, some think that this problem can be resolve by constructing a syncretistic religion which can see the whole as a unity. This will help in full comprehension of the Real. Byrne admits that individual traditions as aspects of an overlapping encounter with the one reality does indeed because pluralism views the diverse religious traditions overlapping encounters with the one ultimate Reality, it does not mean that as traditions they can benefit by sharing common insights, saints, and other features. But this does not also mean that it will end up in syncretism. A person can argue that because diverse traditions interpret through different cultural concepts, it results in an understanding of the Real in its varied manifestation; and this heterogeneity and plurality will get eliminated in a syncretistic religion. Therefore, every religion is needed believed and practiced by its followers for understanding the Real as such.

A problem closely associated with the aspectual view is that the followers of different religions understand the Real only through varied cultural concepts already inherent and self-contained in those traditions. But descriptions about the Real are not sufficient knowledge claims about the Real. Therefore, one has to tackle religious skepticism. Byrne clarifies the problematic saying that if pluralism is true, then the plentiful existing doctrinally loaded interpretations of the nature of the transcendent Reality and liberation/salvation become necessary and flawed. They are inevitably flawed because with regard to the nature of the problem they cannot assert truth with certitude to cohere in detail with the Reality they denote. A pluralist is ignorant about which detailed, first-order beliefs are wrong/true. An individual thinks that they are all highly uncertain.

According to Byrne, this kind of criticism can only be set aside partly. He views pluralists as "mitigated sceptics". We cannot establish the validity of any religion. Therefore, we acknowledge recognize this fact, and the standpoint of agnosticism is best, if we admit the interpretation of religions. There is a cognitive aspect in the doctrinal claims proffered by religions. For example, the claim "Jesus is the Son of God", helps us in giving form to religious experience and praxis. The can also possess some metaphorical truth and referential success. But this does not mean that the claims of religion are objectively and indubitably true. [13]

So far, we have discussed some traditional approaches of how a follower of one religion should understand other religions and their followers. Now, we can examine the views of Hick. In the context of the varied existing religions, Hick suggests three kinds of responses by an individual, as follows: (1) one can adopt a skeptical stand when we consider myriad divine beings worshipped in the different religions. We can regard all these Gods and belief systems as having arisen from an anthropomorphic projection and deep unconscious wish-fulfilment. (2) we can adopt the exclusivist view, characterized by Hick as dogmatic because the dogmatic view maintains that except one's own religion and its divine beings, all the other religions are illusions. For Hick such an exclusivist view is dogmatic because the reason behind adopting one religion is the same as that belonging to another religion. The sole reason for viewing one's religion as different from other religions is very human, but not satisfactory because it is one's own religion. Hick rejects the exclusivist and the inclusivist religions as dogmatic, because it is wrong to consider religions other than one's as inferior. As opposed to Exclusivism and Inclusivism, Hick advocates Pluralism, because for him, each religion identifies the existence of the divine in human beings each puts a path forward salvation/redemption as an equivalent for the self-transformation of human beings. Therefore, in Hick's view the response of human beings to a plurality of religions is as follows.

Hick's religious pluralism must be examined based on his declaration that all religions are equally valid and true. If we consider the claims of diverse religions as stating the real/final truth; then the fundamental claims of all religions cannot be true. This is responsible for the conflicts based on the basic tenets postulated by different religions. Now the question, which arises, is: how Hick true in his declaration that all religions are equally valid and true?

Hick's understanding of religions is founded on the unity of the theological principles advanced by the religions with corresponding soteriology; and the capacity of the soteriology to initiate a self-transformation from ego-centric to pure consciousness. When Hick proclaims the validity of all religions, his claim is based on the view that all the paths to liberation/salvation recommended by diverse religions work equally well. But, what then are we to do with the varying theological claims of all world religions? Is the ultimate true and divinity and, the Allah of Islam, the Christian Trinity, or the unitary Yahweh of Judaism, or Lord Krisna Lord Shiva Goddesses Sakti of Hinduism- from among the manifold Gods seen in the diverse world religions? Hick cannot defend himself by admitting, that all the above and polytheism too are true, because the Gods of different religions are equally venerable; because as seen earlier Hick's own view is that each religion declares its Goddess/God as the only creator or cause of all finite existence.

According to Hick, divinity transcends all the individual Gods/Goddess of different religions. But the problem is with our incompetency to comprehend divinity in a form of immediacy. The, divine Reality is accessible to human beings only through individual God we worships as Allah, Yahweh, Krisna, Siva and other personal gods through whom human beings belonging to different tradition and culture have interacted with the absolute Real. Experience of the Divine through a multitude of deities constituting the religions are the very modes of the Real Divine. And, it is this feature that has enabled followers to experience the Divine through various personal deities, and accomplish self-transcendence. In addition to the individual personal goddesses/gods who express the Divine for human experience the impersonal Absolute also functions in the same way, i.e. there is manifestation of the Reality through intuition/ realization/ experiential knowledge of Brahman. Therefore, the validity of diverse religions originates from the fact that, these individual personal gods and the impersonal Absolutes are the bases of devotion and religion which manifest the Ultimate.[14]

Hick's religious pluralism is based on a transition to the divine centric from the self-centric, which according to him is a fundamental principle on which all are based on great religions. But, Hick is not the first thinker to advocates religious pluralism, because Paul Tillich too had similar views. For Tillich, the highest divine Reality is "Being-itself" or the "Real-it-itself" as discussed in his later writings. Hick's aim is to distinguish the "Real as experienced by us from the Real in-itself or ultimate Reality. Hick views personal deities as the objects of one's worship in religion and these are the Real as experienced by us. Now, the concept necessitating clarification is the nature of the transcendent divine Reality? What is it that can be stated about the Ultimate divine reality-the Real-in-itself? Hick admits that nothing significant can be said about it. For Hick, the difference between the Real-in-itself and the real as experienced and thought by us, is determined by the positive and negative descriptions which we ascribe to the real-as experienced and thought by us, i.e., the individual's personal deities, but these cannot be applied to the Real ascribed in itself/Real-as-it is.

The experience of Reality acknowledged by different religions, either as personal gods or impersonal absolutes is equally significant for human self-transformation. But, it is very difficult to explain how the absolute Reality which by its nature is indescribable and ineffable can initiate our self-transformation. Due to this aspect, we can even doubt the very possibility of Hick's the Real-in-itself. As mentioned earlier, Hick's Real-in-itself does not possesses a positive substantive-teleological, or a negative substantive-non-teleological. Many philosophers can reject such a concept on the ground that it is incoherent because for them what is existence or real must possess one or the other above cited feature. One can deny the presence of a few attributes in something. But, it is impossible for something to be lacking in and devoid of both the properties. For example, the quality of not being or being a pencil. Therefore, it is evident that the Real as understood by Hick is lacking in having the attribute of being a pencil. Hence, it should possess the negative attribute of not being a pencil. But, Hick's theory is lacking in both these characteristics? If a person agrees with Hick and admits "neither the quality of being a person, nor its opposite" it can be stated that Hick's view is incoherent and reject it.

So, Hick's view that all the gods of different religions or the one God known by different names, are invalid; what then has Hick to endorse about the existing gods of diverse religions? Without an explicit endorsement, Hick states that the deities/gods are "projections of religious imagination." The gods appear as human creation in one's encounter with the ultimate Reality. These are not merely mental projections of one's inner of inner psychological needs, because such beings really do not exist. As insisted by Freud and other skeptics, they are the effects of a creative imagination corresponding to human experience of ultimate Reality transcending all linguistic descriptions the Real-in-itself.

This Chapter reveals the difficulties and tension posed by the presence of manifold religions in the world. We have particularly examined the supposed attitude of a follower of one religion towards others and other religions as a whole. To summarize we can say that Exclusivism is spontaneous and natural religious response. Sometimes it is detrimental to social ethos. But, Inclusivism, negates these difficulties by endorsing the validity of all religions.[15]

There is a need for further clarification. There are two mutually contradictory exclusive views in Pluralism. (1) One view admits the equality of all religions and rejects the possibility of any religion as a universally normative. (2)The other view, proposes a theory which can be recognized as universally valid. However, the first form requires a normative conception of religion. But, it simultaneously denies the possibility of any such theory. Therefore, the first form looks incoherent. A universal theory is proposed by the second form. But this very formulation negates any interpretive function to the theory. Therefore, this form also looks incoherent. Thus, it will not be wrong to say that a coherent pluralistic theory is impossible: the presence of a theory of world views is impossible, which by itself is not an interpretation of a world view from some perspective. We can conclude by stating that inclusivity has a stronger claim than pluralism in the present discussion. The pluralistic position implies incoherence.[16]

Hick's contends that we should view all the world religions as proffering efficient means for liberation/salvation, and that all of them involve altruism. Therefore, all of them are 'true' in that they facilitate self-transformation. But the common propositional view is that all religions cannot be true because they admit opposing tenets and principles. But Hick declares that these mutually conflicting views should not be seen as problems, because there is no need for an individual to follow these abstract and historical doctrines for practicing sincerely a religion altruistically.

Hick opines that the followers of different religions understand the Real through accustomed cultural concepts along with their historical, social, and political dimensions. Hick further declares that there is no interpretation or understanding of the Real, which can accurately convey about the Real. This is so because one cannot ascribe any substantive, to the Real which is neither many nor one or impersonal or personal. According to Hick, to express it differently, Muslim view about the personhood of Allah is not different from the Hindu view about the impersonal nature of the Real; i.e. while Muslims maintain that it is wrong to say that Allah (the Real) is personal, they are not any far from the truth admitted by the Hindus that the Real is impersonal. For Hick both the claims are equally faulty. But, it is irrelevant, when we consider the fact, that both of them practice altruism. [17]

4.4. RELIGIOUS RELATIVISM

Religious Relativism involves adhering to one's own dogmas, but recognizing the central questions generated by Pluralism. For Joseph Runzo, a prominent proponent of religious relativism, it means 'hen fideism' as derived from the Greek word *hen* (one) and the Latin word *fide* (faith) – whereby the validity of a religion is relative to the world-view of its adherents.

Runzo upholds that different religions result from diversities in religious experience and mutually conflicting truth claims; and that this diversity is itself based on unique *Weltanschauungen*, which are mutually conflicting, if not contradictory to the others. For Runzo, the incompatible *Weltanchauungen* arise from a plurality of phenomenal divine realities experienced by the followers of these religions.

This standpoint states that a person's world-view, (i.e. the cognitive web of one's interrelated beliefs, rational thought-process and concepts) influence how one experiences and understand the Real. Moreover, corresponding to the diverse worldviews, there are mutually conflicting but individually sufficient, groups of conceptual –schema, or relative truths. This means that the validity of a religion is determined by its adequacy to correspond appropriately with the worldview of which it is a part.

According to Runzo religious relativism is more advantageous than Hick's pluralistic hypothesis: (1) it provides a better explanation of the actual cognitive beliefs entertained by the followers of the world religions, because it maintains the dignity of the different religions by admitting their differences as significant, and real, and (3) it does not reduce to mere image the reality of the Real as pluralism unintendedly does. Rather, it retains the Real as the direct object of religious faith.

Furthermore, it claims that it has several other advantages over aspectual pluralism: (1) it facilitates a better understanding of the actual cognitive beliefs of the followers of the great religions, (2) it furnishes a conceptual, and adequate full description of Reality which is distinct from a schismatic view, and (3) it does not require new, syncretic system for an understanding of the Real. Despite these advantages over pluralism, there are significant objections against religious relativism.

Even though relativism provides a better comprehensive explanation than pluralism about the actual cognitive beliefs of the followers of religions, it still falls short of their actual beliefs. For instance, Muslims the truth of Allah as the only God is unrestricted by the historicity of the belief or is true only in the Islamic *Weltanschauung*. But the truth of Allah as projected by the *Quran* is objectively and unequivocally true. Moreover, Allah is the one and only true God for everybody regardless of *Weltanschauung*; and this is a applicable for the Christians and the Jews also. Therefore, this emphasizes the fact that the followers of these religions have been mutually exclusivist instead of as relatives.

The second objection of the critics against religious relativism that it is logically incoherent because the opponents state that truth cannot be consistently maintained as individualistic as upheld by the relativists. But, although it is a fair assessment of "subjectivism" which states that truth is not objective and universal but is relative to one's own worldview; this critique cannot prevent the notion of *hen fideism*, because *hen fideism* contends that the relativization of truth based on a worldview of a culture and not on an individual plane.

As noted at the beginning of the Chapter, religions proffer truth-claims about our basic notions, on human existence, rebirth, ultimate Reality etc. There are also diverse approaches for understanding the truth-claims of religions: according to the atheists, religious truth claims are totally false whereas the agnostics argue that it is impossible to know whether religious claims are true or false. But the relativists while asserting that each religion has its own truth absolutely reject the idea of objective universal truth regarding religious claims. There are pluralists who maintain that religious truth-claims are true in that its followers understand and experience the ultimate Reality through enculturated concepts. The exclusivists believe in only one true religion through which a person can attain salvation; they reject the truth-claims of all the other religions as false. The inclusivists are content in affirming that while one's own religion is privileged (in some sense), the other religions contain important elements of truth. [17]

Some American philosophers, working on problems closely associated with religious plurality, are examined subjectivity/subjectivism- objectivity/objectivism. While endorsing the objectivist emphasis, for e.g., in empirical science, they criticize objectivism in varied forms like scientism, and metaphysical realism, presently known as the God's eye-view. Although they admit the significance of relativism in its forms, they do not consider it as a viable medium of solutions. They favour for a kind of pluralism including a form of inclusivism.

Hilary Putnam is associated with eliminating the dichotomy between the subjective and objective views of reason and truth. Many philosophers, according to Putnam, admit the mimetic theory of truth as correspondence to mind-independent facts, while others view systems of thought as relative and subjective.

Putnam's understanding of truth and rationality blends harmoniously the objectives and the subjective components. Putnam identifies this approach as internal or pragmatic realism. His realism is different from external or metaphysical realism. According to metaphysical realism, the world is composed of mind- independent objects about which only one true and exhaustive knowledge exists. In this "God's eye view," truth means correspondence between objects and worlds. But, internal realism, considers truth not as correspondence; but as rational acceptability, which is an ideal coherence of our experience and beliefs. Therefore, this view rejects "God's eye view": Objects do not exist independently of conceptual schemes. But, signs can denote objects, both being internal to the scheme. It is meaningless to question whether one's concepts correspond to or refer to something unrelated to concepts, because experiential knowledge in itself involves conceptual schema. An important outcome of Putnam's internal realism is the scope for pluralism, the existence of "equally coherent but incompatible conceptual schemes which fit our experiential beliefs equally well." Putnam states that many internalist philosophers admit that there is more than one 'true' theory about the world. Such pluralism does not admit metaphysical realism which asserts the existence of the "one true theory" or "God's eye view." According to his model model of truth and rationality are dependent on one's value system; which in turn is determined by one's presumptions about human nature, universe, society, theology and metaphysics. Finally, Putnam maintains that relativism is not the correct alternative for metaphysical realism and 'God's eye view' due to incoherence, inconsistency and self-negating nature of Relativism. Through a complex argument, called 'transcendental argument', Putnam shows that rationality is transcultural and that there is a convergence towards an ideal or limit concepts of truth and goodness.

Putnam's views have implications for religious inclusivism and pluralism. His most significant point is related to the possibility of a plurality of equally consistent but incompatible conceptual schemes which suit our experiential beliefs equally well. This possibility is in accordance to his formulation of internal realism and its implication of conceptual relativism. Putnam's theory appears as a foundation for the affirmation of the initial forms of pluralism the congruence of the great world religions, in their description of truth. Furthermore, Putnam's rejection of the 'God's eye view' 'one true theory' of the world implies that second form of pluralism based on a universal theory is illegitimate. But, a question that spontaneously arises is whether a theory of pluralism is absolutely required for the possibility of pluralism, i.e., a universal theory which explains and interprets the manifold conceptual schemas or religious outlook. For Donald Davidson the intelligibility of a plurality of conceptual schema is based solely on the existence of a 'common coordinate system on which to plot them'. Therefore, the possibility of pluralism implicitly involves a theory of pluralism regarding 'God's eye view'. Moreover, Putnam assertion that some conceptual schemas are better than others, and that a transcendental argument is conducive to transcultural rationality, which converges towards an ideal or limit concepts of goodness or truth. These suggestions explain his transition from the first form of pluralism towards a second form of pluralism which is the same, as seen in moderate inclusivism.[19]

CHAPTER - 5

IMPLICATIONS OF RELIGION

5.1. RELIGION AND SCIENCE

Science and religion play major important roles in the present world. Approximately 85% of the world's population entertain religious beliefs and belong to some religion, whose effects have great global impact. Similarly, the outcome of science too has widespread effects across the globe. Be it the market streets of London, the serene hills of the Himalayas, or the dense forests of the Amazon, the gadgets of science and technology- e.g. the radio, television, mobile, computer, etc. have become an indispensable part of our daily life. Also, science has been adopted in religion and several ardent religious followers are also scientists. Since centuries, religion and science have existed symbiotically. However, at times, both these domains are also at loggerheads with each other. The argument of Galileo with the Roman Catholic Church on whether the earth or sun is a stationary celestial body is an often quoted famous example. The problematic fact is that religion, in its several forms is irrational and dangerous. Religion, when grounded on a blind belief system can make one forget reason and become irrational, leading to violence and terrorism. Religious faith should be guided by reason. The highest level of rationality is science.[1]

The disciplines of science and religion are getting more and more important to human beings in the contemporary society. They are two great disciplines, which, when combined harmoniously, can confer all-round benefits for humanity. But, unfortunately, since the last few centuries, the relationship between the two has not been quite healthy. From the twentieth century, a new approach has been noticed and the representatives of science and religion are beginning to identity close inter-relation between these two branches of human knowledge. They are slowly recognizing that science and religion can heartily embrace each other, without endangering the cause which they represent, and work for the good of humanity. It is being realized more and more by both that there are elements in science that religion can adopt in order to fortify itself, and elements in religion that can deepen and strengthen science.

I shall here dwell on some points of contact and discuss the methods and results of both disciplines against the background of the unity and totality of knowledge in the light of a synthetic approach and vision of Swami Vivekananda - an outstanding spiritual and intellectual luminary of the modern age, who worked successfully to bring about this great consummation. In the two words "equilibrium" and "synthesis", Vivekananda's constructive genius may be summed up. He embraced all the paths of the spirit: the four Yoga's in their entirety, renunciation and service, art and science, religion and action from the most spiritual to the most practical. He was the personification of the harmony of all human energy.

The civilization in which we live today is a product of a discipline of the human mind known as science. When we study science closely, the way in which great scientists have applied themselves to this pursuit, we can identify two aspects: (1) pure science, which tries earnestly to understand the truth of experience through a dispassionate inquiry; and, (2) applied science, in which the truths discovered by pure science flow as inventions for the technical enrichment of human life. These two, science as *lucifera* and science as *fructifera*, science as *light* and science as *fruit*, always go together. Knowledge leads to power, and power leads to control and manipulation of the forces of nature, to enable human beings modify one's life and environment. Every new discovery in pure science, at some point of time gets converted into applied science, for controlling and manipulating the forces of nature. And the result as revealed in recent history is the world-wide technological civilization of today. It is highly interesting to see how the human mind through science is able to wrest from nature hidden truths to usher in an extra-ordinary age of nuclear science and space travel.[2]

But, when we go deeper into science, its limitations become evident. For example two branches of science, *viz.* physics, including astronomy and biology, have given us a vast body of knowledge regarding the nature of the universe and human kind. Till the end of the nineteenth century, physics was warped in its final judgements. It saw materialism and mechanism reigning supreme in the universe. There was then cocksureness in its pronouncements! But, in the twentieth century, an element of humility becomes discernible in the attitude of the great physicists of the age. In the nineteenth century, knowledge was not deep enough, and scientists looked only at the surface of things. But, the discovery of radioactivity and insight into the nucleus of an atom, have explored the severe limitation of our knowledge regarding the Truth of the external world. Science confesses today that it deals only with the appearances of phenomena and not with the Reality behind the appearances. Great modern physicists tell us that science has revealed only the outer aspect of phenomena, and that behind the observable universe, there is also an unobservable universe. This is a great acknowledgement about the limitations of science and its methods. Science deals with phenomena perceived by the senses or by apparatuses aiding the senses. Although the senses reveal little they tell us that there are realities behind the sense-world determining it and controlling it. Science restricts itself to an understanding of the observable universe and controlling its energies for use by mankind.

A similar situation exists in the science of biology. After studying the different aspects of the phenomena of life, it arrived at the great theory of evolution from which it drew certain conclusions a form of materialism which equated human beings with an animal, and both with a machine. Today, scientists declare that they were not happy titles that Darwin chose for his famous books *The Origin of Species* and *The Descent of Man*. The science of (1) physics with its thoroughgoing materialism and mechanistic determinism, and (2) biology with its newly discovered evolutionary theory and its domination by the materialistic outlook of science and the scientists have shattered the nineteenth century human faith in religion and spiritual values.

In addition to this, religion was attacked by great social idealists and revolutionary social thinkers like Karl Marx. It was the period of industrial revolution. The idealists asked: if there is God in an extra-cosmic Heaven - why is there so much suffering in this world? Why are millions starving? And why are thousands of little children made to slave in factories and workshops for the gain of a few capitalist exploiters? This kind of inequality, oppression of one human beings by another in the presence of an all-powerful God, is something which we cannot understand, explain or witness. Marx therefore characterized religion as the soul of soulless conditions, the heart of a heartless world, and as the opium of the people.

The result was that, by the end of the nineteenth century: religion and faith in God and eternal verities ceased to be the ruling ideas of modern civilization; the power of religion to influence human thinking and conduct disappeared; human beings lost the fear of God; and more especially the fear of the Devil! Religious dogma had upheld the latter more than the former as conducive to moral control of human action and belief. But scientific spirit destroyed not only faith in the Devil but along with it, also faith in God as well. These were treated as primitive superstitions not worthy of entertainment by a modern civilized human being. Modern science views religion as a dangerous error in the beginning and as a harmless illusion in the end.

But the two great World Wars, and various economic and political, crises that occurred in the twentieth century, chastened the attitude especially of thinkers those in the scientifically advanced countries of the West. Social thinkers became less certain about their remedies for human ills. Even great scientists began to feel and express that science, as understood and pursued by them, was not sufficient. Einstein said: 'Science can de-nature plutonium: but it cannot de-nature the evil in the heart of man.' That is not its function. Most scientists will agree today that science alone cannot ensure human happiness; it can only create conditions for happiness; but, it cannot ensure that human beings will be happy and content. That is not the function of science as understood by the positive sciences like physics, biology, etc., but, it is the domain of another discipline, the science of the inner nature of human beings, which is the true meaning of religion as understood in Indian thought.[3]

The functions of Science are "*science involves the description, explanation, and prediction of events in the physical world which can be checked and corroborated by empirical evidence.* Often the claims made by science contradict the religious claims of religion. Several options have been put forward to relate both religion and science. This chapter will examine three main aspects of science and religion under - conflict, independence, and integration.

Conflict

A way to understand the relationship between religion and science is to view them as conflicting and contradicting each other. Such a conflict has prevailed over centuries, a prominent example this is the became creation–evolution controversy. This conflict e evident in 1860, when the biologist Thomas Huxley (1825–1895; called as 'Darwin's Bulldog' for advocating the theory of evolution) was asked by Bishop Samuel Wilberforce (1805–1873) whether he claimed simian descent by way of his grandfather or grandmother. The unscrupulous reply of Huxley was that he would be much happier to have descended from an ape, rather than one, who would have destroyed the truth and brought in confusion. The conflict was mainly caused by a misunderstanding of the limitations and roles of religion and science. On one hand, the scriptural literalists, who followed the sacred scriptures (in this case, *Bible*) gave a historic and an accurate account on the creation of the universe and all the living phenomena such as plants, animals and the primitive humans. The story of creation preferred by the scriptural literalists conflicted with the evolutionary history of living beings. Both cannot be true and scripture supersedes science. On the other hand, the scientists who acknowledge the conflicting accounts of science and scripture believe in naturalistic evolution and claim that no religious background is required to understand the origin of life. The conflict approach faces several challenges. Firstly, scientific materialism (sometimes referred to as *scientism* holds that the only possible way to acquire knowledge is through science and that matter is the only reality. However, this can be treated more as a philosophical assumption, rather than as a scientific conclusion. Secondly, several studies on religion and theologians declare that sacred scriptures could not be regarded as textbooks of science. It is wrong to believe that these can provide information on geology (e.g. age of earth), biology (e.g. evolution of humans from lower life forms) or astronomy (e.g. sun being a stationary or a moving celestial body). According to Galileo and like-minded thinkers, information on God and His creation are revealed in both "*The Book of Scripture*" as well as "*The Book of Nature*". Since both the books are from God, they cannot conflict one another. But, since science and religion have their own distinct and unique spheres of reality, they cannot provide a complete picture of reality. Hence, one is led to the next option. [4]

Galileo is a notable ex ample of the so-called conflict between science and religion. In vain did Galileo try to show that the old Ptolemaic, earth-centered system of astronomy was inadequate and that it should be replaced by the Copernican, heliocentric cosmology? In solemn congregation the assembled theologians declared:

> "The doctrine that the earth is neither the center of the universe nor immovable, but moves evenly with daily rotation, is absurd, and both philosophically and theologically false and at least an error of faith".

The next great example for science - religion conflict can be seen in the reaction of the Churches to Darwin's theory of evolution. The reverberations of this conflict have not completely died down. Indeed, the implications of evolution for science, religion, and philosophy have not yet been solved. And when this idea of evolution is carried into the field of religion itself, the battle that subsided after the Tennessee trial flares up again in an even more violent form. The idea of a continuously evolving body of religious insight shocks the orthodox mind. Organized religion has never seriously attempted to integrate the idea of evolution-biological evolution, mental evolution, and social evolution-into the core of its thinking. It has pinned the theory of evolution securely onto its garment of theology; but it has seldom examined what might be inferred from the evolution of religion. This well-established idea that religion should be static in a dynamic universe explains why there is so much Churchianity and so little Christianity, so much administration and so little inspiration. The great church campaigns today are campaigns to raise money-to bring people "back to the Church". If the Churches had vision, in a mystical or a scientific sense, the people would go "forward" to the Churches, not back to them. But the Churches today are as lacking in mystical experience as they are in scientific knowledge.[5]

Independence

Another option to understand the science and religion relation is to treat them as independent domains of thought and practice. This perspective appears to provide an irenic picture between science and religion as both are distinct; and, therefore, never contradict each other. Although there are various forms of expressing the independent view, two expressions, viz. Protestant neo orthodoxy and linguistic analysis are very prominent. Karl Barth (1886-1968), who was a prominent figure in the 20th century Protestant Neo-Orthodox Movement believed that God is transcendental and could not be known, until and unless He discloses Himself. Such a disclosure cannot occur via scientific methods or discovery. Instead, it can happen only by a divine revelation, which happens *via* the initiation of the Spirit of God. Religious scriptures can throw light on such a divine knowledge, although they must not be interpreted literally. This is so, because the scriptures are seen as recordings of revelatory events by humans and are hence considered fallible. On the contrary, according to Barth, science can provide useful information on the empirical world. But, it cannot deliver religious knowledge. The aims, methods of investigation and the subject matter of these two large domains are completely dissimilar. Another method of viewing independence approach is by expressing the two domains in different languages, in each of their own unique set of functions. Logical positivists, who were a group of scholars in the mid Twentieth century, observed that a claim which can be verified empirically only could be regarded as true and meaningful. In this light, views of religion seemed meaningless. Although logical positivism was only short-lived for various reasons, a later movement emphasized the analysis of language, called as linguistic analysis. Religious and scientific language has their own distinct and unique aims and functions, proclaim the linguistic analysts. While the aim of a scientific language is "prediction and control in the natural world", religious language intends to recommend a way of life, elicit a set of attitudes, and encourage conformity to particular moral codes.

As some call it, science and religion have their own unique "language game", and both the games neither interact nor conflict with each other. It becomes clear that the independence approach has no warfare involved, unlike the conflict approach. As said by Ian Barbour had religion and science been completely independent of each other, there would have been no possibility of conflict or a constructive dialogue. Life is not divided into distinct compartments; but it is a whole and inter-connected. The independence approach maintains that religion provides no information about the nature of the world, just as science makes no judgments on religion. However, it appears to be not true. For instance, according to three major theistic religions, God brought the universe into existence and God is actively involved with the created beings (e.g. healing of the ill, introducing plagues, parting the sea, etc.). Empirical facts serve as the basis for believing in the existence of a God a supernatural Creator. At times, the claims made by science and religion are at conflict with each other. The independence approach attempts to bifurcate these two large domains and rejects a unified interpretation of the same. To have a complete picture of the world, it becomes important to unify these two domains, for leading us to the following, final method of interpretation.

Integration

A third method to understand the relationship between religion and science is by integrating the two fields. While the integration approach admits the conflict between science and religion on the one hand, it also considers the unique roles of the two domains on the other hand. Although several ways of integration have been attempted, two leading methods have been outlined. Natural theology is an important attempt, which deciphers the existence of God from signs in nature. Several findings from physics and other disciplines of science furnish fresh reports to natural theologians, backing up their claims on God's existence. It is important to note that it is possible that both natural science and natural theology could lead to a same object, irrespective of their unique objectives and approaches. For instance, the cosmic constants of a universe might make one appreciate and lead him/her towards the perfect Creator of this universe, who is believed in the theistic religions. Furthermore, Richard Swinburne (1934) has also put forth Bayesian/Probabilistic Arguments to prove God's existence and resurrection of Jesus.

Another viewpoint of the integration method is to have a systematic synthesis of science and religion. A noted example of an attempt to merge both religion and science into a cohesive and a comprehensive metaphysical system, that is consistent with theories of modern science (e.g. theories on relativity and evolution) is the "process philosophy", which corroborates the eminent works of American philosophers, such as Alfred North Whitehead (1861–1947) and Charles Hartshorne (1897–2000). The process thinkers believe that the views of the ancient and medieval times are static, and that the substantial properties of objects are replaced by dynamic events. The basic notion of a process thought is that all the existing objects are characterized by a process. This notion is promoted by the Buddhist doctrines of interdependent arising and *anātman*, according to which substantial entities do not exist; rather all the events are interconnected. According to the process view, God is also in a process. Process thinkers refute the classical theistic opinion of God, which says God is absolute, omnipotent, omniscient; One Who is beyond time and space, etc. Rather, the process thinkers view God as dipolar – (i) a primordial nature, ordering the world, and (ii) a consequent nature, interacting and continually changing the world. The integration method attempts to develop new prospects of merging religion and science. The two major domains overlap each other in many important contexts and taking the dialogue further would require the recognizing importance of each domain in human and non-human life. It is also important to understand that scientific theories are not static, but they grow with the evolution of humankind.[6]

Science is connected with the natural world, whereas religion is concerned with a supernatural existence. Science is confined to only sensible forms of perception, while religion deals with super-sensible phenomena. Science involves collection and organization of data, based on a hypothesis and when the hypothesis is verified to be valid, it becomes a scientific law. The laws of science laws are based on some theory; and the theories are backed by data. Moreover, the theories and laws are framed to predict, regulate and control the future. This ability to predict and control the future events made science acceptable to the civilized community. On the other hand, religion deals with one's personal achievement and an autobiographical narration about the supernatural experiences of the mystics. Such mystic accounts cannot be subjected to public verification. This led Whitehead to regard religion as solitary.

Although religious experiences are gained solitarily, they are also beneficial for the entire society and also the world. Society would crave to know the insight of a solitary man in a forest or a cave or under a banyan tree. For instance, Lord Buddha found what the *Ajivikas*,

262 heretical sects, whom the Brahmins of the time were endeavouring to find out. When Buddha started preaching, many wise people accepted his teachings with gratitude. Jesus had the vision of angels and archangels, when he was on the cross. He also visualized a future sect of people, who would acknowledge and follow him as their master and the Lord. Hence, a solitary meditator usually has the vision of the ideal community as well as the whole society in his mind. Religion thus has a significant place in the society of India than those of the West because Indian society often involves various castes and communities. On the contrary, in the modern society, science has been favoured over religion and the latter is regarded as a personal matter of the people. This is so, because science has given us the ability to fight against natural disasters such as floods, droughts, famines, etc. It also entices people by its various future promises.

As for religion, even though science has conquered nature, it has not helped us conquered the inner self of a (wo)man. Without the morals of religion, a person can misuse the science and technology invented to destroy humankind and the whole world. The weapons of destruction are very powerful, that they could totally wipe off life from the surface of the planet. Politicians all over the world are much attracted to money and power, that they use religion as a toy. As a result, several clashes and communal riots have occurred worldwide, based on caste and creed. Yet, the true believers do not support the use of religion in politics. They believe that the right use of religion can help us conquer evil. This kind of a belief existed in ancient India, as chronicled by the Greeks.

Even though science can control nature, to some extent; scientific laws are not always certain. Although the laws of science have a high degree of probability and validity, some form of doubt always lingers about the future investigations of nature. This is perceived to be a healthy attitude of science. On the other hand, devoutly religious people tend to be very dogmatic and their firm psychological conviction is purely subjective. Exclusion of doubt forms the core of religious belief. No firm theist would proclaim that he/she would accept the reality of God, if one gets a first rank or a job. A theist totally surrenders and accepts God in one's mind and soul, whole heartedly. A theist would say, "Even though He slays me, I will cling to Him still". However, unfortunately, of late, this attitude has bred a lot of fundamentalism, causing so much hatred among the followers of different religions. It is also this same attitude, which creates conflict between religion and science.

Another major difference between science and religion is that, while religion is matter of emotional neutrality, a scientific truth prevails despite the likes/dislikes of a scientist. For instance, even though Charles Darwin was a pious Christian, he has to accept the evidence and doctrine of organic evolution, against his Christian belief and theory of creation.

In contrast, a mystic often sees the vision of what he most ardently wanted to see. Ramakrishna reported the seeing of Ma Kali or other *mythological* Gods, while a Christian mystic would see Christ. There is neither a unanimity nor novelty in the freshly observed mystic reports and these are often the same which have been observed in the past. However, science keeps on observing and adding new facts in various fields. People of deep thought, including scientists have long maintained that religion and science are two distinct spheres, which are not in conflict with each other. Religion is grounded on values, whereas science is based on facts.

It is beyond doubt that science has established various facts in the world. However, one that cannot be sensed does not fall under the purview of science. But, the scientific facts follow a specific order and are interconnected by uniform happenings called "scientific laws". Only those laws that can be repeatedly publicly verified are held as true, and the others are rejected as false. Hence, a scientist relates the facts and proposes the laws with sincerity, which is deemed as a moral virtue. A scientist also prefers to have a simple, rather than a complicated explanation. This could be seen as an aesthetic value. Based on the above statements, a scientist could also be counted as an artist. It is essential to note that moral and aesthetic values occur incidentally in scientific pursuits and these values are not directly pursued in science.

A scientific statement needs to be unbiased, predictable and reasonable. Therefore, the language of science is quantitative and anything that exists as a number. For example, one added to one is two, whether one likes it or not. Thus, scientific statements are exact. On the other hand, religious statements are qualitative and evaluative. For example, the statement "God is love", "*Brahman* is without any difference within or without", etc. From a modernist's perception, science has bestowed humankind with amazing inventions. Due to science, one is able to land on the moon, computers have made our jobs simpler, and one can see and chat with a far-off relative through one's mobile. Scientific investigations are very thrilling and rewarding, that its status is elevated to that of a religion. This is known as scientism, according to which the methodologies and the results obtained in science are absolute. Nowadays, mystic and Yogic disciplines are also treated as scientific, as they undergo various physical and mental exercises, and there are definite stages of development, with uniform results.

Irrespective of how rigorously a religion is followed and how meticulously the steps and stages of meditation are followed (e.g. the eightfold Yoga and the fourteen stages of *Guṇasthāna*), the result of such a discipline can never be reliable, like that of science. This is because a scientist strictly remains emotionally neutral with regard to scientific facts. In contrast, in the case of religion, the entire personality is involved in observing and recording the religious experience similar to mystic experience. Therefore, as Martin Buber correctly observed, science involves the relationship of 'I-It', with regards to facts, whereas religion deals with 'I-Thou' relationship in communicating with God. While the mind works in science, the entire personality is actively involved in religion. Yet, these two major spheres do not contradict each other. A scientist tries to gather pearls of facts, while a religious seeker endeavours to become a pearl himself/herself. According to religion, knowing is less important than becoming a product of value, worthy of entering Heaven. Cognition/understanding is of immense importance for understanding spirituality. Therefore, it is clear that knowing and becoming are complementary to each other just as science and religion are complementaries.[7]

5.1.1. Vivekananda's Point of View

Modern civilization has overrated science and technology just as the older civilization had underrated it. There is need today to view science in perspective – the perspective of total human knowledge and welfare. This is one of the several vital contributions of Vivekananda to modern thought. Dealing with the complementary character of eastern contributions to religion and western contributions to science, he said in a lecture on 'My Master' delivered in New York in 1896:

Each of these types has its grandeur, the mingling of these two ideals. To the oriental, the world of spirit is as real as to the occidental is the world of senses. In the spiritual, the oriental finds everything one wants or hopes for; in it one finds all that makes life real to the individual. To the occidental he is a dreamer; To the oriental, the occidental is a dreamer playing with ephemeral toys, and he laughs to think that grown-up men and women should make so much of a handful of matter which they will have to leave sooner or later. Each calls the other a dreamer. But the oriental ideal is as necessary for the progress of the human race as is the occidental, and I think it is more necessary. Machines never made humankind happy and never will make. One who is trying to make us believe this, will claim that happiness is in the machine; but it is always in the mind. That individual alone who is the master of one's mind can become happy, and none else. And what, after all, is this power of machinery? Why should a man who can send a current of electricity through a wire be called a very great man and a very intelligent man? Does not nature do a million times more than that every moment? Why not then fall down and worship nature?

Here is the meeting point of science and religion, as revealed by Indian thought; for religion, as expounded in Vedanta, takes up the investigation of the mystery of experience where the positive sciences leave off. This 'Man the Unknown', man as the subject of experience, is its special field of investigation. According to Swami Vivekananda: 'the bold search beyond consciousness. Consciousness is limited by the senses. Human beings must go beyond the senses, in order to arrive at the truths of the spiritual world. There are people who have succeed in going beyond the limitations of the senses. They are called *ṛṣis* (seers of thought), because they have directly perceive spiritual truths. Indian thought recognizes that both religion and science are valid disciplines in the pursuit of truth. India admits the view of

Eddington about the spiritual kinship between science and religion: 'one can understand the true spirit of science and religion only when seeking is placed in the forefront.'

India's thinkers never saw any contradiction between the two, unlike the scientist and theologians of the West. Such contradiction and conflict are the result of a narrow view of both science and religion which, however, the modern West is struggling to discard. Many students of science, not to speak of laymen, have vague and rather confused notions about what science means. The same is true about religion. To an ordinary person, science means no more than gadgets like radio or television, or other material objects conferred on humankind by scientific and technology. Students of science generally identify it with the several branches of science such as physics, chemistry etc. But we have to turn to the great scientists themselves to learn what science is; and from them we learn that it is the pursuit of Truth –of Truth hidden in the facts of nature, in the data revealed by the senses and the data derived from experiments. It is a sincere, critical, detached study of experience, by which confused data are reduced to meaning and orderliness and brought under control. According to Karl person:

The classifying fact, recognizing their sequence and significance, is the function of science. Forming an unbiased judgement based on these facts, is the characteristic of a scientific frame of mind. Science thus understood is not restricted by any particular body of facts; it is characterized as an intellectual attitude. It is not bound by particular methods of inquiry because it is basically sincere critical thought, which accepts conclusions only when they are supported by evidence. There is scientific method involved when: (1)a businessman meet some new practical problem, (3) a lawyer sifts evidence, or (3) when a statesman frames a constructive bill.

Religion as developed and understood in the West was, in its aims, methods and data, opposed to the spirit of rational seeking and investigation. It was understood as something finished and ready-made, which people had to believe – a creed or a dogma, a frozen piece of thought, and unquestioningly accept. That was why it fiercely collided with the advancing tide of science with its spirit of seeking and rational inquiry. In India, on the other hand, religion has always been understood as a matter of seeking, inquiry and verification, like any other branches of science. This is a statement that is corroborated by the great *Upaniṣads* of ancient

India and the works of Swami Vivekananda during our own time. Tracing the recurring conflicts of science and religion in the West to the absence of this broad approach, Vivekananda said that we all know the theories of the cosmos according to modern astronomers and physicists. At the same time we all know how miserably they falsify the theology of Europe; how scientific discoveries have blasted its stronghold; and how theologians have at all times attempted to ruthlessly put down and stifle these researches.

A study of the *Upaniṣads* reveals that the subject of religion was approached in ancient India in an objective and dispassionate manner. The aim of the study was to disclose Truth and not dearly embrace pleasing fancies and illusions or idolize tribal passions and prejudices. In his lectures and discourses Swami Vivekananda often expounded the scientific approach to religion as practised in Indian thought. In his lecture on "Religion and Science" he says that experience is the only source of knowledge. In the world, religion alone becomes science for one who has no surety, because it is not accepted as a science of experience. This should not happen because are people called mystics who teach religion from experience. And, these mystics in every religion speak about and teach the same Truth. This is the real science of religion.

In a lecture on "*Cosmology*" Swami Vivekananda declared that "there are two worlds: the macrocosm and the microcosm, the external and that internal. We get truth from these realms through experience. The truth obtained through internal experience is psychology, metaphysics and religion. And, the truth known through external experience, are the subject matter of the physical sciences. A perfect truth is one which is in harmony with the experiences of both these worlds. The microcosm must authenticate testimony to the macrocosm, and vice-versa; physical truth must be supposed by the internal world, and the internal world must have its evidence in the external world.

Therefore, the seers of ancient India studied the physical life of (wo)man, and also the physical universe surrounding humankind in a scientific manner. They made an in depth study of (wo)man and human nature as revealed to one's consciousness, awareness, emotions, ego and one's sense of selfhood. These latter phenomena too were investigated. Every discovery in domains adds to human knowledge about the truth of the mystery of the external world.

The techniques of investigation in the realm of religion and the positive sciences are similar involving gathering facts, classifying them and studying them dispassionately to expose the law or laws underlying them. Such knowledge confers to control over the phenomena concerned; and its application mitigates human suffering and enriches the quality of human life. This kind of approach towards religion, as a rigorous scientific study of the truths of inner life, was made by the great seers of ancient India. The insights which they got were re-tested and expounded by subsequent thinkers for gifting to posterity the invaluable heritage of a holistic and dynamic and a scientific tradition in the field of religion. This foundational basis has enabled Indian spirituality the test of time. This feature also explains its accommodative attitude towards modern science, and its pride in the noteworthy achievements of this related discipline developed by the contemporary West.

According to Romain Rolland 'real Vedantic spirit', does not begin with a system of preconceived views. It has absolute freedom and peerless courage amidst religions in terms of the facts for examination and varied hypotheses poised for coordinating. Unrestricted by priestly order, every person has been free to seek wherever one desired for a spiritual interpretation of the cosmos.[8]

Swami Vivekananda has discussed how Vedanta and modern science resemble each other in tempered spirit and aim. Both are spiritual disciplines. Amidst the physical phenomena, the two reveal several points of contact. The basic position in the cosmology of science and religion is what Swami Vivekananda calls "the postulate of a self-evolving cause"; Vedanta calls it as Brahman the universal spiritual principle.

The *Taittirīya Upaniṣad* defines Brahman in a majestic utterance which will be welcomed by every scientific thinker: *Yatho va Imāni bhūtāni jāyante; yena jātani jīvanti; yat prayānti abhiṣamviśanti; tat vijijnasasva; tat Brahmeti* –Which mean that forms which all these beings are born; by which, being born, they abide; into which, during dissolution, they enter – seek to know that; that is Brahman'. To a modern scientist, it is a material reality, the basic material or stuff, in the terms of the astrophysicist Fred Hoyle. And both admit the theory of evolution, cosmic and organic.

Commenting on this spiritual similarity between modern science and ancient Vedanta, Swami Vivekananda at Chicago, in his speech at the Parliament of Religions in 1893 said that manifestation, and not creation, is the work of science presently. A Hindu will only be too see that what was told in Vedanta in more stronger is going to be taught in more forcible language, and with more evidence by the latest conclusions of science.

Even though modern science does not accommodate any spiritual concept or reality, many scientists of the twentieth century, e.g. biologists like Teilhard de Chardin and Sir Julian Huxley, have tried to dilute the materialism of physical science and secure a place for spiritual experience in the world of science. During the 19tht century Thomas Huxley, a collaborator of Darwin, had questioned associating science with fixed dogma such as materialism, and rebuked materialism as an "intruder". In the 20th century, this objection has come from great physicists themselves. Sir James Jeans discovered that the final picture of the cosmos arising from twentieth century physical science will be one where matter was completely negated with mind reigning supreme and alone. According to Astrophysicist R. A. Millikan materialism is a philosophy of unintelligence. If 20th century physics is abandoning thoroughgoing materialism, twentieth century biology overtakes it in this direction. Modern scientific thought is undergoing of a silent spiritual revolution with the acknowledgement of mind and consciousness, and the need to admit what Jeans calls as "a new background of science". Julian Huxley and Chardin perceive the spiritual nature of the world in organic evolution and biology in the theory of evolution. Chardin identifies a within of nature different from without of nature as revealed by physics and astronomy. For Vedanta the *within* is *pratyak* and the *without* as the *parāk* of nature.

The recognition of the significance of the within in modern scientific, has brought it closer to the Brahman of Vedānta. The synthesis of the within and the without is what India accomplished in its Vedanta centuries back as *samyak jñāna* complete knowledge. According to Indian philosophy on reality there is no difference between the within and the without. These differences created only for facilitating study and research. Science the diverse branches of the positive science are only varied approaches for explaining the same reality; all such approaches merge into a grand science a unified science of the cosmos culminating in the science of Brahman, the Total Reality. Thus Vedanta viewed its science of Brahman (*Brahmavidya*), signifies the totality of Reality, material and non-material.

Swami Vivekananda in his lecture on "*The Absolute Manifestation*" delivered in London in 1896, stated that 'science is moving towards the Hindu view arrived through at study of the mind, via metaphysics and logic. The west started from external nature, but now has arrived at the same conclusions. Searching through the mind one at last arrives Oneness, at Universal One, the Internal Soul and Essence, the Reality of everything.[9]

Religion thus understood has a message for all humankind. Science with its technology can construct a house, and equip it all kinds of gadgets; the Welfare State can prefer with everything for making a person happy. A person can name one's house attractively as "Happy Home" etc., but none of these can guarantee that a person can dwell in that house in peace and happiness because being happy and content is determined by another kind of knowledge and discipline – arising from religion. Positive sciences can create a comfortable external environment, but the science of spirituality alone can confer create a conducive internal environment, for actualizing total fulfilment in one's life. But presently this is not the case with modern civilization presents. Amidst technological civilization there is internal impoverishment even through there is wealth, power, and pleasure. There is sorrow and tension, unending doubt and uncertainty. Drunkenness, juvenile delinquency, drunkenness, suicide, and other kinds of miseries are increasing because a person is not inwardly at peace with oneself and the others and discontentment resulting from sensual *Weltanschauung*. Indian seers foresaw these miseries since millennia.

That human beings can (through their technical skill) roll up the sky like a piece of leather; but there will still be unending sorrow for them without realization of the Luminous One within'. A hundred years ago Schopenhauer said that: all men who are free from want and care, after having cast off all their other burdens, have now become a burden to themselves'. The *Svetāsvatara Upaniṣad*:

"*Yada carmavat ākāśam vestayisyanti mānavah*;

Tada devam avijnaya duḥkhasyanto bhavisyati"

Presently, humankind is facing a major crisis. This crisis cannot be solved by more science, or technology, material comforts more socio- political solutions, except through cultivation of the science of religion, its understanding and practice. One must always remember that religion is not mere talk, doctrines or books, but realization it is not learning but being.

It is in this sense that India has understood religion. And it was this idea of religion that Swami Vivekananda proclaimed in West and the East through his powerful voice. The aim and end of religion, as our ancient seers put it, is on the experience, (*anubhava*), of God, Reality through the steady growth if one's spiritual awareness. That is the touchstone of religion. The spiritual growth of an individual begins when one practices religion. Consciousness expands sympathy and empathy widens, and one can feel that one is becoming a better human being. The strength that results from such inner growth and development alone can nullify the negative the energies produced by the progress of science. Such a person alone has the strength and wisdom to convert the chaos of life into a pattern of happiness and general welfare. If religion is eliminated from society, what remains is naive barbarism. Ancient culture was destroyed by barbarians bred outside that culture. But modern civilization, if allowed to continue will be destroyed by barbarians bred within the modern society. This miserable situation can be avoided by cultivating "Christian love" in ourselves for the others, according to Bertrand Russell; or a little more altruism, according to Pitirim Sorokin of Harvard University. This love results from the practice of religion, as described by Swami Vivekananda and other great world teachers. For Vivekananda: "Religion is the manifestation of the divinity already in human beings".

According to Swami Vivekananda, a *mahātma* (Great Soul) is one whose heart bleeds for the poor, otherwise one is a *durātman* (wicked soul)". The function of religion is to enable the finite man reach out to the infinite man. No other discipline can bestow this knowledge which ensures eternal life. It will transform human beings from stagnating as brutes. Sensual pleasures are not the goal of human life, but wisdom (*jñāna*). A person enjoys the intellect more than an animal enjoys its senses. But, we see that a human being enjoys one's spiritual nature more than one's rational nature. Therefore, the highest wisdom is spiritual knowledge which will confer bliss.[10]

5.1.2. Einstein's Point of View

Einstein the famous scientist was highly-aware of the importance of religion. He strongly believed that there is a healthy relationship between religion and science. He rejected the idea of deducing religious beliefs from science, and also the popular notion that science has got nothing to do with religion. Exposing a superficial concept of science and religion. Einstein declared that a non-reciprocal relationship exists between science and religion, and that science is much dependent on religion, and not vice-versa.

(1) Several works of Einstein reveal that there are at least six ways, through which religion contributes to science. These reveal what religion meant to Einstein. The contribution of religion to science is experimental in nature. There are no logical and hard and fast rules, according to Einstein, for correlating factual experience and the theoretical laws of physics. True religious belief in the perfect order of reality bridges the above-said lacuna.

(2) A major contribution of religion is the epistemic thought that it confers. Without religious insight, thought will remain impoverished and incomplete. According to Einstein it is very important to correlate the varied faculties of understanding. For him, all our moral leanings and tastes, sense of beauty and religious instincts are tributaries helping reason accomplish its highest achievements.

(3) The role of emotions in understanding the mystery of art, science and religion is emphasized by Einstein. Since everything is vision-oriented, gaining religious insight will enhance scientific sensitivity. According to Einstein, the mysterious is the most beautiful thing we can experience. It is the fount of all true art and science. A person lacking in emotion is a stranger, incapable of appreciating anything. Such a person is as good as dead because of lack of vision. This vision is, for Einstein, an insight into the mystery of life.

(4) Einstein highlights the motivational role, where the soul is on a scientific quest to attain peace and balance. This religious motive can at times, express itself via philosophy or art, besides being prominent in a scientist's creativity also. According to Einstein human nature has always attempted to create for itself a simple and synoptic image of the

surrounding world. Which accomplishing this it tries to create a picture which will yield some tangible expression to what the human mind perceives in nature. That is what a poet, a painter, a speculative philosopher a natural philosopher, engage in each in own way. Within this picture one places one's own soul, so that one can rest and be equipoised amidst responses to everyday life.

(5) without the support of religious beliefs, scientists will not be able to continue for long, in their quest of the elusive science and intelligibility of all the existents. The inspiration which gives scientists the power to pursue their purpose despite countless failures is the cosmic religious sense which grants them this power.

(6) Einstein discusses the role played by religion in his life. Even as a child, Einstein was always interested in going beyond the hopes and strivings of human life. This helped him to develop a deep sense religiousness, which got abruptly halted when he was twelve. And was replaced by physics.

In the above instance Einstein has used the word "religious" to indicating something that was commonly or conventionally regarded as religious. In all the other contexts, he uses "religion" to refer it's something more fundamental and inclusive. It indicates a rational understanding of religion. According to Einstein, religion is concerned with human attitude towards nature at large and positing ideals for the individual and the society and better human relation. Most religions function by postulating and organizing basic values for practice in life, as in poetry, art, science, philosophy, and other disciplines.

Einstein upholds that while religion influences science, science does not influence religion. He was firmly convinced that human values determine and direct our search for science and reasoning, but human values, are not determined by science. For Einstein science is systematic aimed at thinking finding regulative relations between sensing experiences? Hence, the function of science is to only help us achieve the ends. Therefore, its role is merely to function a servant, and not as a master.

It is clear that morality has no roots in science. Einstein answered a critic by saying that these are moral foundations for science, but not scientific foundations for morality. He also did not admit a sharp contrast between religion and science. He emphasized the power of morality and religion and the powerlessness of science.

Explaining the non-reciprocal relation between science and religion, Einstein maintained that the results of science are totally free from religious and moral considerations, although the individuals who have made achievements of science entertained religious conviction that the world is perfect and capable of being known. Therefore, inspiration and guidance are important features which are totally different from the results of science. Hence, Einstein rejected the view that there is reciprocal influence between science and religion. His writing reveals that his awareness about the powers of science, are positive, while some are negative. On the positive side, Einstein admits that science profoundly and positively influences the essential and basic values of people in the physical world. Science changes one's focus from worldly activities and strengthens one's morale. He was firmly convinced that all effort to reduce ethics to scientific formula will collapse. On the other hand, he was doubtlessly sure true that scientific study of the higher phenomena and general interest in science are very valuable towards a worthier leading human being evaluation of spiritual phenomena. The recognition of this fact by Einstein indicates the difference between the theory of science about it contents and the influence of science while formulating the theory itself. Einstein also upholds that the science of contemporary physics will have a positive influence on religion. Admitting Max Planck is views, Einstein states that

"modern scientific theory is moving towards a kind of transcendental syntheses wherein the scientific mind can function harmoniously with a human being's religious instincts and a sense of beauty. He admits that the picture of the physical world professed by the theories of modern science is similar to a great painting or bit of music that draws out the contemplative spirit, a feature of religious and artistic pursuit".

But science can also negatively affect religion. Einstein states that the "abrupt ending" of traditional Christianity of his youth was mainly the result of his study of books of science which made him conclude that Biblical stories cannot be true." Einstein was also aware about the conflict between science and the conventional religion as practised in the Synagogues and Churches. He says that traditional religion depicts God as interfering in the activities of humankind and by functioning as a moral judge, rewarding or punishing one's actions. But science rigidly follows natural laws ignoring the traditional role of God. Intervention by God is a feature of "religions of fear" in as Einstein's terminology, and it is meaningless to as follower of science who admits an absolutely determined universe. Similarly, moral praise or blame, and related rewards or punishments, too are equally questionable that A God rewarded and punishes is unthinkable, because a person acts according one's requirements. The conflict between traditional religion and science becomes very clear. Anyone who admits the laws of causality will reject the view that God interferes in the sequence of events in the world as an absolute impossibility. The religion of fear or the social-moral religion cannot impress a person of science who admits causality. Hence, the reason why Churches have suppressed science and have punished its supporters for rejecting religious beliefs.

But this struggle between science and religion can be misunderstood; Einstein's concept of religion is different from the traditional definitions put forward by various institutions. The real battle is between different religions. There are many people, who admit traditional religious concepts, such as fear and morality; and others who admit "cosmic religion." According to Einstein, a "cosmic religion" recognizes four interconnected concepts: (i) human aims and desires, (ii) order in nature, (iii) understanding one's individuality as imprisonment, and (iv) a grand intuition that all existents display a perfect unity.

Einstein, has stated that he experienced the urge of cosmic religion as a child, and that he initially followed a traditional Judaism, from which, he directed his attention to physics, to liberate himself from the "chains" of the "merely personal". His faith in cosmic religion strengthened him when during the "long years of lonely work" he made immense effort to understand "even a small glimpse of the reason revealed in the world" like Newton, Kepler and other scientists. According declares that cosmic religion disclosed his soul' "center of gravity", and enabled him to remain in rest and equilibrium" a state hankered after by human beings. Einstein transcended the beautiful mysterious depths of the universe through cosmic religion, being rewarded with overwhelming emotions of awe and ecstasy. Cosmic religion helped Einstein bind all his faculties together in his epistemology, by focusing his "reasoning faculty toward its highest achievements." Cosmic religion made Einstein the eminent physicist understand that the universe, space-time, and thereby helped him interpret quantum mechanics.

There are also many ways, other than Einstein's approach, regarding science and faith. There are several alternative religious insights and perceptions for realizing the ultimate values. Einstein's belief on cosmic religion may not be adequate enough to converge all the religious and moral views together. Values and experience matter more in religion, than in science. we cannot take for granted that Einstein supported the above statement. Einstein, in fact taught us not to believe that the "wild speculation" in science would be irresponsible or beyond any reason. According to him, "a theory is good if its premises are simple, relates many diverse phenomena and is very extensive in its scope of application." Einstein's religious views have to be evaluated carefully through suitable criteria. In this light, a cosmic religion too can have its own limitations just as any other human invention.[11]

There is a universal guiding field of influence, closer in nature to the cosmic fire (intelligent energy) of the Stoics than to the Creator in the orthodox interpretation of Genesis, which gives coherent form to the evolving realities in space and time. Human consciousness, in its awareness, properties, and purposiveness, is an expression or epitome of this cosmic energy (or form producing field). The only knowledge (wo)man has is human knowledge, and no final truth can come into his range of understanding greater than the capacity of the human mind to recognize and utilize in a given age. There are no revealed religions disclosing final and absolute truth. Science, religion, and philosophy express human effort to know this large cosmic field of influence. Therefore the only "true" religion is the one that encourages this continual creativity of (wo)man in his search through science, the arts, philosophy, and religion for means of one's deepest vision of the meaning of the evolution of life on earth and the development of mind in society.[12]

5.2. RELIGION AND MORALITY

Religion is a holistic response of human being to what is considered as the ultimate concern. Religion involves three main aspects of human life - cognition, conation and affection. Cognition is concerned with scientific pursuits, conation is related with morality, and affection is expressed in art forms. Just as the trilogies of the mental aspects are inseparable, religion too exists together with science, morality and art. The religions of ancient civilization were closely bound with science, morality and art. But, with the dawn of thought process, the three dimensions became distinct and autonomous as represented by "art for tart's sake", and "Morality for morality's sake".

There are different about the relation between religion and morality.

1. Religion and morality are interdependent and inseparable.
2. Religion is independent of morality.
3. Morality is independent of religion and is an autonomous domain.

For modern times, morality is an autonomous discipline. The concept of God in morality has been holly debated. "Freewill is a very important concept in morality. Modern philosophers like J.L. Mackie and A. Flew argue that God could have granted freewill to humankind and ensured that their free actions do not stiffer any moral lapse. But Alvin Plantinga questions this view, because according to linguistic conventions, free acts cannot be determined. Hence, God, Who created (wo)mankind could not have granted freewill to (wo)man and prevented one's free actions from becoming moral violations.

The five commandments (*yama*) of Yoga are comparable with the *Panca Mahavratas* five great vows of Jainism. And these five vows of morality are emphasized by most Indian religions. This shows that religion and morality are interdependent and inseparable in traditional religions. Interdependence means the mutual relation and dependence between religion and morality. According to Freud, a person can abandon aggressive and cruel behaviour in the name of God as shown proven by the head-hunters of the Khasi and Garo hills, after they became Christian, and interact with their neighbours with due respect. This shows clearly that religion incorporates the values of morality for a good life. Even if morality viewed as an independent and autonomous domain, religion is associated with morality.

According to Kant and R.B. Braithwaite, God boosts morality psychologically in an individual. Since, performing duties is not easy, Kant recommends that duties must be viewed as "divine Commands".[13]

The religion-morality relation is a popular topic often debated and discussed on philosophy. During ancient times, the Prophets of the *Old Testament* preached the practice of justice and righteousness before God. In the process, they directly and indirectly criticized diverse popular beliefs about Gods, according to their standard. This raises questions regarding the relation between one's conduct in life and traditional belief in God's nature and His functions.

A Greek philosopher Xenophanes identified a discrepancy in the relation between belief in Gods' nature and the ideals of good life: ... Homer and Hesiod say that the gods engage in activities which according to (wo)men are disgraceful: adultery, stealing, deceit, etc. for e.g. the actions of *Indra* on Indian mythology. Religion-morality relation has become a very important in philosophy, since the period of Enlightenment. And it is also very different from the ideologies of the Christian theologians. Kant has argued that morality must be viewed as an autonomous discipline independent of theology, religion and dogmatic metaphysics. He was interested in separating morality from psychology; relativity and a camouflaged self-interest which could endanger threaten morality or transform it into something else. He strictly adhered to a view, consistent with perfect character and holiness. Consequently, the idea about being rewarded/ punished according due to one's actions as per Deism, Protestantism and Catholicism contradicted his ideology. Hence, he rejected the doctrine of moral heteronomy, according to which morality is determined by extra-moral motives. During Kant's period, there was a controversy between a positive or historical religion and a rational or natural religion. This can lead one into believing that an ideal good life can either (1) displace positive or historical religion as old superstitious thought or (2) transform it into for providing the required emotional mental-flame for leading, a life of reason and following the religious commands obediently. Many philosophers regarded morality as totally independent of religion and metaphysics. Secular culture modern times are predominantly based on the principles and values of the Enlightenment. It admits the above-cited view. Many contemporary thinkers maintain that "scientific" morality is based on biological, sociological and psychological aspects; and, that therefore morality and religion are distinct. This is so because; true morality can be arrived at as a product of scientific analysis, an independent of religious superstitions. From an analysis of the relationship between God's nature and moral or good standards, a problematic arises having two marked features: (1) it may be based on a theological query, or (2) it may come under the scope of modern philosophy.

The first problem is concerned with the moral nature of God and moral standards like righteousness and mercy. The second, problem is related to the extent to which morality (that determines man-man relationship) is based on a person's pursuit of religion and conventional traditions of religion. Viewed from a literal sense, the concept of "relation of religion to morality" falls under a theological framework. For attaining an in-depth understanding of the subject, the second problem must be examined in detail because it is about structural organization and the problems experienced by modern culture. It is very essential to differentiate a religious concern and morality because these two words are not synonymous, related to a loose context of "values" which is totally different from "facts". Although the terms can be related, they are remarkably different. This distinction can be best-explained in the context of the typical contrast that exists in Western Christianity – between "pietistic" and the "atavistic" sects. The first group focused emphasized the religious aspect of experience, whereas the second group focused mainly on morality and maintaining an idealistic relationship between human beings, which often exceeds the frontiers of religion. The former acknowledge the final destiny of (wo)man approach God with devotion and trust, admitting the great difference between (wo)man (due to sinfulness) and God, necessitating reconciliation or salvation. But the latter reject this view.

The prevalent contemporary concerns on ultimate questions and foundations, greatly determined by the vast historical data and evils can be summarized as: "What is an individual supposed to do? What is one's duty?" The concern of this context is related with the affairs and activities of this world; for e.g. economic and social justice, caring for the weak and the poor and attempts to create a state of affairs a kin to the perfect Kingdom of God. Both the above analyzed tendencies prevail as mutually excluding concerns (because atavistic aspects are found in pietistic philosophy and *vice-versa*) in the Judeo-Christian tradition, as visible in the religion of the *Old* and *New Testaments*. These two poles deal with religion-morality relationship.

Morality is primarily founded on principles governing social conduct and ethical life of human beings in a society and often strives to reconstruct society, through ideals. Strictly speaking morality deals only with the human society (including its imperfections) and it is indifferent to issue about the ultimate destiny of the populace and the society, who/which practice its dictates.

Hence, it is clear that morality deals with righteous conduct of human being and maintaining order in the society. It is totally different from religion because it not concerned with the destiny of humankind who pursue religious knowledge to eliminate their doubts, despairs and fears. Religion is preoccupied with providing a final resting place for the soul and transcends the physical universe and time. Religious attitude demands trust and contemplation, whereas other hand, morality is concerned with the problems of this world in shilling and ensuring order in the society. Morality does not care or know about phenomena beyond the material universe. It is only interested in refining the society, according to its codes and norms.

After discussing the distinguishing features of religion and morality, it is important to examine the main problem, regarding the relation between religion and content and the form of morality? We have to clarify the relation between moral standards and moral passion; faith in God as the basis and goal of life and the ultimate destiny of human beings. This question is very important because people now believe that religion has nothing to do with morality. Due to progressive scientific advancements, people believe that intelligence can answer complex questions of human being, who attempt to perfect their lives through rational consciousness, motives and consequences. Since the concept of religion, viewed as foundational for morality, the term "religious morality" is interpreted as authoritarian in spirit and as opposed to the freedom of inquiry. It constitutes the basis of the doctrine of "scientific" morality, which is not only possible but is also very essential. It challenges the authoritarian view regarding motives and norms for isolating those who reject morality due to religious views. Unfortunately the possibility that morality can require non-authoritarian religious basis is not even recognized. To solve this problem it can be said that Kant and all the others who had faith in the autonomy of morality are right. As stated by Spinoza, a good life is not a means to another thing, for it is the supreme end itself. Hence, morality must be granted autonomy to eliminate the fear of a tyrannical deity or persecution by Church while analysing human behaviour. It is also not restricted by the considerations of material gains and worldly successes. Goodness in life is opted for its own sake, which implies that morality is autonomous.

The question about religion-morality relation persists. It is very important to clarify the extent to which morality is dependent on the norms and concepts of historical religions, and the desire to abandon wealth, pleasure and worldly success, for leading a life as taught by moral principles. The *Biblical* answers these questions clearly, according to which the ideals (content) that govern human beings in a society are from the divine and love of God (form) empowers a problem to lead a good earthly life. It also exhorts an individual to be merciful and just, imitating the qualities of God. Human beings are also expected to express their love because love too is also a quality of God. Ultimately, it is the love of God which dwells in hearts of His devotees, that grants motivation and inspiration to all human efforts. The religion-morality relation can be seen in the first epistle of John: which says that a person says that he loves God, but hates his brother is a liar. According to this, the principle of ensuring order among human beings is mainly determined by a religious aspect - God's nature. The author disapproves human beings who proclaim their love for God, but do not love their fellow beings. Therefore, it is God's nature which determines the code for conduct, but the love of God decides the motive. But some philosophers who reject this view uphold that an authoritarian nature of God creates fear of divinity or ecclesiastical retribution or both; and that therefore human conduct is not derived only from the love of God and that religion functions as the basis of morality. From a historical, standpoint this view cannot be totally rejected because there are many instances of distortion of religious morality, where the main motive of love is substituted by non-personal or an external authority. But, one should not immediately reject the religious basis of morality, just because there is scope for perversion. Love of God functions as the basis of a good life, as revealed by *Old Testament* Prophetism and classical Christianity, where a good life is described as one turned towards centered around God. Therefore, the view where love of God is regarded as motivating force of morality is free from subjugation or fear of any external authority. On the contrary, in this case, a person's conduct is determined by the core motive and attitude, whereby he/she desires to lead a good life; and their function in society is an expression of individuality and personality, deeply rooted in God. Genuine morality must be autonomous, i.e., not dependent on any external force or authority affecting personality or reducing the status of a "good life" to "a means" towards achieving something. All protests against religious morality can be justified only if their religious foundation gets converted into an authority. However, an autonomous morality is not a phenomenon totally lacking in religious basis. Both prophetic Judaism as well as classical Christianity declares that morality sans religion is absolutely impossible.[14]

Only the main features in this regard can be conveyed here, but the following relations between the two are defensible:

1. Any criticism of a prevailing state of affairs in a society is possible only when there is an implicit or explicit assumption of the unconditional validity of standards with reference to which such criticism is made. All evaluative assertions about human actions (except rigorously descriptive assertions) contain or imply a proposition like "such and such ought to be done," and the term "ought", or some logical equivalent. This is applicable, when for example; one is criticized for not loving one's neighbours, not pursuing clarity in philosophical activity or for not employing intelligence when engaged in daily affairs. Moreover, the standards used to inform us about what ought to be done (some idea about a good life) cannot and, does not remain neutral with regard to question which is truly a religious one: the query about and concern for (wo)man's ultimate destiny as a creature in His world. Just as moral criticism presupposes moral standards, so also moral standards themselves presuppose views about the ultimate destiny of (wo)man. A study critical discussion of all about human conduct having assertions that are evaluations will show that a claim like "The fact regarding (wo)man's ultimate destiny is such and such" is presupposed. This truth has been ignored to such an extent that is scandal our for moral philosophy. The best way of indicating this is by drawing one's attention to the ethical writings of Dewey, who calls himself a naturalist, and is an opponent of the view of religious morality. But, it is evident to anyone who criticize his views that a proposition like "The ultimate" destiny of (wo)man is to manipulate one's destiny through

technology or intelligence is presumed throughout. This presumed is an assumption about the fundamental religious question, and that it operates as an ultimate premise in Dewey's views is evident from the fact that not only is there no proof for it anywhere, but it is not ever raised for discussion. Finally, no view about, the good life, no serious doctrine about what (wo)man ought to do, is ever possible sans some view about the ultimate human destiny; and such a view carries with it a religious element. The above discussion shows that morality is inseparably related with religion.

2. A great danger affecting morality is that it may get reduced to ideology or a coat for the hypocrisy of self-righteousness. A morality that is not rooted in a reality transcending itself gets inescapably corrupted because it does not posit a judge beyond its own commands. But, a morality, based on a love of God, which is religious in nature and one which recognizes the power of God as judge is not vulnerable to such corruption and resulting transformation into an ideology. Such morality rooted in religion admits that it is subject to the same final principle of criticism (divine judgment) through which it judges existing persons and societies. And a morality rooted in that which transcends all times (because it belongs exclusively to no one time) contains within itself its own principle of criticism. Such criticism is brought to bear: (1) subjectively through self-conscious judgment by the followers of that morality, and (2) simultaneously objectively through the medium of historical happenings. A morality not based on religion has a principle of self-criticism because it has no transcendent reference to which it is itself subject and which judges it. This does not mean that in fact, religiously rooted morality has not been corrupted in the past. Such a claim can be made only when ignorant about the truth but, nevertheless, it true that, in addition to establishing the content of morality, religion is the final judge of morality. It exists as an ever present guardian, cautioning about morality of its possible pretensions and helping it to remain free from transformation into ideology.

3. Ultimately, religion provides the inspiration for moral life and simultaneously the meaning and purpose of moral endeavour. A person having morality is according to Royce, like a man serving an ideal master who is always in a distinct land. The servant, who serves

without even seeing the master, can begin to doubt the existence himself master. An individual whose morality is based on religion knows that the Master has full faith in the final purpose of one's action. One's view about the ideal society, Kingdom of God, gives form and content to one's effort to not only regulate one's personal life according to certain standards but also strive for reconstructing the society, according to the likeness of the ideal God's Kingdom. Without a vision, hope, and faith of religion, in such effort is always incomplete. In the above discussed ways' religion is a genuine basis for morality without simultaneously being an authoritarian force behind it necessitating good life through fear. Since it is the fear of authority that critics of religious morality usually condemn (and rightly so), a religious base that negates this danger and simultaneously provides the base without which all morality will get destroyed can overcome the criticism. Morality is uncertain and incomplete without a living relation with religious faith. A recognition of this truth can be quickened of we can ensure that religious morality is devoid of authoritarianism and, that due to reasons given above, morality implies religion; and, when it is not based on religion gets constantly endangered by destruction.[15]

CPSIA information can be obtained
at www.ICGtesting.com
Printed in the USA
LVHW081213241022
731386LV00009B/393